The
TaxFitness
TOP 20% BUSINESS BENCHMARKING SYSTEM

A proven framework for accountants
to deliver high-value advisory services

DARREN GLEESON

Published by Vivid Publishing
A division of Fontaine Publishing Group
P.O. Box 948, Fremantle
Western Australia 6959
www.vividpublishing.com.au

A catalogue record for this
book is available from the
National Library of Australia

Manual information

The book contents are general information only. It is not intended to be taxation, accounting, business, financial, legal or other professional advice and should not be acted on or relied upon as such. Specific professional advice should be sought regarding particular circumstances and requirements, as the information may not be suitable or applicable to specific circumstances and should not be acted on or relied upon. The authors have made reasonable efforts to ensure the content's accuracy and currency, but do not guarantee its accuracy or currency. They will not be liable or responsible if it is not accurate or up-to-date. In no event will the authors or any related entity of those persons, or any of their directors, principals, agents, employees or representatives, be liable for any loss, damage, costs or expense (whether direct or consequential) incurred as a result of or arising out of or in connection with this manual and the content included in it in whole or in part including but not limited to any error, omission or misrepresentation. The authors also disclaim all representations and warranties, including but not limited to the quality, accuracy or completeness of the information of whatsoever nature and warranties of fitness for a particular purpose.

If you have any questions regarding the manual, please contact:

TaxFitness Pty Ltd
6/50 Ladner St
O'Connor WA 6163
Tel: 0412 842 856
Email: darren.gleeson@taxfitness.com.au
Web: www.taxfitness.com.au

Dedicated to Robert C. Camp, the father of benchmarking

Robert C. Camp (1935–2019) is widely recognised as the father of benchmarking. While working at Xerox in the early 1980s, he developed the first formal benchmarking process to help the company regain competitiveness against Japanese rivals. His 1989 book, Benchmarking: The Search for Industry Best Practices that Lead to Superior Performance, established benchmarking as a global management discipline and remains a cornerstone reference for continuous improvement.

In the early 1980s, while working at Xerox, Camp recognised that simply measuring internal performance was not enough. Xerox faced fierce competition from Japanese manufacturers, who were producing higher-quality products at lower costs. To survive, Camp developed a structured process to study competitors, identify best practices, and close the performance gap.

His work culminated in **"Benchmarking: The Search for Industry Best Practices that Lead to Superior Performance"** (1989). This book didn't just introduce a methodology — it created a movement. Benchmarking became a recognised management discipline, a tool for continuous improvement, and a way for organisations worldwide to measure themselves against the best.

From Xerox to TaxFitness

Just as Camp provides business leaders with a framework to measure and improve, TaxFitness brings that same discipline to accountants and their clients.

- **Camp's legacy:** Benchmarking against the best to drive performance.
- **TaxFitness today:** Benchmarking against the **Top 20% of businesses in over 400 industries,** with structured advisory strategies to close the gaps.

Where Camp's system helped corporations like Xerox survive and thrive, TaxFitness applies those principles to the small and medium businesses that form the backbone of our economy — delivered through accountants, the trusted advisors who can make benchmarking practical and actionable.

Why this matters
Robert Camp showed that **knowing your numbers is not enough — you must compare them to the best and act on the insights.**

The TaxFitness Top 20% Business Benchmarking System continues this philosophy for a new era: providing accountants with the tools, data, and processes to transform compliance into advisory services and clients into top performers.

This book is written in recognition of Camp's groundbreaking work and in dedication to extending the power of benchmarking into the world of accounting and small business advisory.

Contents

8. Step 4 – Educate clients

9. Step 5 - Sell service to client

10. Step 6 – From benchmarking to advisory – The two TaxFitness databases

11. Step 7 - Select business advisory strategies

12. Step 8 – Top 20% business benchmarking repor

13. Step 9 – Advisory meeting (report presentation)

14. Step 10 – Implementing strategies

15. Risk management and professional standards

16. Avoiding the common benchmarking mistakes

17. The future of Top 20% business benchmarking & advisory

18. Case studies – Benchmarking in action

1.

Introduction

Purpose of this book

This book has a clear purpose: to provide accountants with a **practical, structured system** for delivering business benchmarking and advisory services that consistently achieve results. Many books in our industry are filled with theory, grand promises, or generic advice. This isn't one of them.

The TaxFitness Top 20% Business Benchmarking System is designed as a working tool — a process accountants can pick up and apply immediately with their clients. It brings together:

- **The Top 20% Benchmarking Database** – real numbers that show how the best in each industry perform.
- **The Business Advisory Database** – proven strategies accountants can implement to help close performance gaps.
- **The 10-Step Benchmarking Process** – a repeatable framework for turning raw numbers into meaningful client conversations and ongoing advisory relationships.

The purpose is not simply to help you produce a report. It is designed to help you create a transformation in the way accountants engage with clients, in the value clients perceive, and in the revenue and reputation of accounting practices that adopt advisory services.

Accountants today face shrinking compliance margins, increased automation, and rising client expectations. The firms that thrive will be those that **step into the role of trusted advisor.**

1

Benchmarking against the Top 20% is the fastest way to identify opportunities, start valuable conversations, and deliver strategies that drive real improvement.

This book exists to make that transition possible. By following the system, accountants can move beyond compliance, build deeper relationships, and generate sustainable advisory income.

In short:

- **Purpose for accountants:** A clear, proven system to sell, deliver, and profit from benchmarking and advisory.
- **Purpose for clients:** Insights, strategies, and accountability that help them perform like the best in their industry.
- **Purpose for the profession:** To raise standards, improve outcomes, and redefine the role of the accountant in small business success.

That is the purpose of this book. Everything that follows is built to help you achieve it.

Hall of fame of benchmarking

Benchmarking has been shaped by some of the most influential thinkers in business, strategy, and quality management. Their collective work laid the foundation for today's structured benchmarking systems — and their ideas remain highly relevant for accountants seeking to transform compliance into advisory services.

1. Robert C. Camp – Father of benchmarking

Robert C. Camp is universally recognised as the father of benchmarking. In the early 1980s, while working at Xerox, he faced a pressing challenge: Japanese copier manufacturers were producing machines that were both cheaper and of superior quality. Camp developed a formal methodology to study competitors, identify the best practices that made them successful, and translate those practices into improvements at Xerox. His process combined rigorous data analysis with practical steps for implementation.

In 1989, Camp captured this methodology in his seminal book Benchmarking: The Search for Industry Best Practices that Lead to Superior Performance. This work not only helped Xerox regain competitiveness but also launched benchmarking as a global management discipline. His framework demonstrated that benchmarking was not about copying competitors — it was about learning, adapting, and improving more quickly.

2. W. Edwards Deming – Quality pioneer

W. Edwards Deming revolutionised the way the world approaches quality, measurement, and improvement. After World War II, he taught Japanese manufacturers the principles of statistical process control and the importance of reducing variation. Companies like Toyota used his teachings to revolutionise global manufacturing.

Deming's philosophy of continuous improvement (later known as Kaizen) and his "14 Points for Management" stressed that organisations must measure performance, identify sources of waste and variation, and relentlessly improve. These ideas became the intellectual soil from which benchmarking grew. His work demonstrated that no process is ever "good enough" unless it is compared against a higher standard — a principle at the heart of benchmarking.

3. Joseph M. Juran – Quality management visionary

Joseph Juran, often paired with Deming, brought a practical, people-focused approach to quality management. His concept of "fitness for use" reminded businesses that the customer must ultimately judge performance. Juran also introduced the famous "Juran Trilogy": planning, control, and improvement — a system-atic framework for driving excellence.

For benchmarking, Juran's influence lies in his insistence on repeatable, structured improvement. He made clear that identifying best practices is meaningless unless organisations have a process to adopt and sustain them. Many modern benchmarking frameworks mirror Juran's trilogy: plan the comparison, measure the gaps, and implement the improvements.

4. Michael Hammer – Father of business process reengineering

Michael Hammer shook the business world in the 1990s with his call for business process reengineering (BPR). He argued that incremental improvement was not enough in the face of global competition — companies needed to redesign their processes from the ground up radically.

Benchmarking played a critical role in BPR. By studying best practices from world-class organisations, Hammer gave companies a blueprint for how to "start over" and leap ahead. His famous book Reengineering the Corporation (1993) showed that organisations could not just automate old processes; they needed to benchmark and adopt entirely new ways of working.

5. Tom Peters – Excellence evangelist

Tom Peters, co-author of In Search of Excellence (1982), popularised the idea of learning from the world's best companies. While not a technical benchmarking framework, his work made "excellence" a mainstream goal and encouraged managers everywhere to ask: what are the top performers doing differently, and what can we learn from them?

Peters emphasised customer focus, innovation, and people-driven performance — themes that still resonate in benchmarking today. His book became one of the most influential business texts of all time, helping to move benchmarking out of academic or quality circles and into the executive suite.

6. Michael Porter – Strategy guru

Harvard's Michael Porter is one of the most cited thinkers in business strategy. His concepts of competitive advantage, five forces, and the value chain provided businesses with powerful tools to analyse themselves against competitors.

Porter didn't frame his work as benchmarking, but his ideas made benchmarking inevitable. By breaking down the value chain into activities (production, marketing, logistics, etc.), Porter gave organisations a way to compare specific parts of their business to industry leaders. His strategy frameworks remain the backbone of industry benchmarking, helping businesses not just compare numbers, but also understand where advantage is created.

7. Philip Crosby – Zero defects advocate

Philip Crosby became famous for his philosophy of "zero defects" and the bold assertion that "quality is free." He argued that doing things right the first time saves more money than fixing mistakes later.

Crosby's emphasis on measurable standards and clear performance expectations fed directly into benchmarking. His four absolutes of quality — conformance to requirements, prevention, zero defects, and measurement — all align with the logic of benchmarking. By showing that quality improvement should be quantified and managed, Crosby reinforced the idea that organisations need benchmarks to define what "good" really looks like.

8. Paul Niven – Balanced scorecard expert

Paul Niven helped popularise the balanced scorecard — a performance management system that measures organisations from four perspectives: financial, customer, internal process, and learning/growth.

Niven's contribution to benchmarking lies in connecting

strategy execution with measurement. The balanced scorecard ensures that benchmarking is not just about operational numbers (such as cost or efficiency), but also about strategic alignment. His work made benchmarking part of an integrated system for managing performance, linking day-to-day numbers to long-term strategy.

9. Carla O'Dell – Knowledge & benchmarking leader

Carla O'Dell, as CEO of the American Productivity & Quality Centre (APQC), institutionalised benchmarking on a global scale. Under her leadership, APQC created vast databases of benchmarking data and facilitated cross-industry best practice consortia.

Her work ensured that benchmarking was no longer limited to internal company efforts or single industries. Instead, businesses could access global best practices and measure themselves against peers worldwide. O'Dell also linked benchmarking to knowledge management, highlighting that the real value of data lies in how organisations capture, share, and apply it.

10. Geary Rummler & Alan Brache – Process alignment experts

Geary Rummler and Alan Brache brought process alignment into the benchmarking conversation. Their influential book, Improving Performance: How to Manage the White Space on the Organisation Chart (1990), showed that organisations often fail not because of individuals, but because of poorly designed processes.

They emphasised mapping processes, defining performance measures, and aligning them with organisational goals. Benchmarking became a way to determine whether processes were delivering the proper outcomes compared to those of the best-in-class. Their approach is especially relevant for service industries, where intangible processes drive customer outcomes.

Why this matters for accountants

Together, these thought leaders shaped benchmarking as both a discipline and a practice. From Camp's structured methodology to Deming's focus on measurement, Porter's strategic lens, and O'Dell's global benchmarking databases — the path is clear. Benchmarking is about comparing with the best, identifying gaps, and taking structured action.

For accountants, the TaxFitness Top 20% Business Benchmarking System takes this global legacy and applies it directly to small and medium-sized business advisory services. It makes world-class benchmarking principles accessible, actionable, and profitable within the accounting profession.

History and evolution of benchmarking

Benchmarking is not new. The idea of measuring yourself against the best and learning from them has existed for centuries. Armies compared tactics, merchants compared trade routes, and artisans compared techniques. But benchmarking as a formal business discipline really took shape in the 1980s — and it all started with Xerox.

Xerox and Robert Camp – The beginning

In the early 1980s, Xerox was in serious trouble. Japanese copier manufacturers, such as Canon and Ricoh, were producing copiers that were cheaper, better, and faster. Xerox, once the undisputed leader, was losing market share rapidly.

Enter **Robert C. Camp.** Tasked with finding out how Xerox could compete, Camp didn't look inward — he looked outward. He developed a systematic process for studying the best practices of competitors and even companies in other industries. By comparing processes, costs, and performance levels, Xerox identified areas where it was lagging and what needed to be changed.

This wasn't about copying competitors. It was about learning, adapting, and building something more substantial. Camp called this new discipline benchmarking. His 1989 book, Benchmarking: The Search for Industry Best Practices that Lead to Superior Performance, became the foundation text for benchmarking worldwide.

The quality movement – Deming, Juran, and Crosby
While Camp was formalising benchmarking, the broader quality movement was already underway. Thinkers like W. Edwards Deming, Joseph Juran, and Philip Crosby demonstrated to the world that businesses must measure, compare, and continually improve their performance.

- **Deming** taught statistical process control and continuous improvement (Kaizen).
- **Juran** stressed systematic planning, control, and improvement.
- **Crosby** promoted "zero defects" and measurable standards.

Their combined work provided the intellectual foundation for benchmarking: if you can't measure, compare, and improve, you can't compete.

The 1990s – Expansion into strategy and process
Benchmarking didn't stay inside quality departments. In the 1990s, it moved into strategy and process improvement.

- **Michael Hammer** pushed business process reengineering (BPR) — radical redesigns of processes, often fuelled by benchmarking against best-in-class companies.
- **Michael Porter** gave businesses frameworks like the value chain and competitive advantage, which made benchmarking a strategic necessity.
- **Tom Peters** popularised In Search of Excellence, encour-

aging businesses to study what great companies were doing differently.

This period showed that benchmarking wasn't just about efficiency. It was about strategy, innovation, and learning from the best to leap ahead.

APQC and global benchmarking

By the mid-1990s, benchmarking went global. Organisations like the **American Productivity & Quality Centre (APQC)**, led by Carla O'Dell, built vast databases of best practices and created benchmarking consortia across industries.

Instead of companies benchmarking in isolation, APQC enabled organisations to share data, learn collectively, and apply insights more quickly. Benchmarking evolved from a company tool to a global knowledge-sharing discipline.

The modern era – benchmarking for everyone

Today, benchmarking has moved beyond Fortune 500 companies and manufacturing giants. Technology, data analytics, and AI have made it possible for any business to compare itself to the best.

But here's the reality: while large corporations have used benchmarking for decades, small and medium businesses — the lifeblood of our economy — have been left behind. Most SMEs never realise how they compare to the best in their industry, and most accountants fail to provide that insight.

That's where this book and the TaxFitness Top 20% Business Benchmarking System come in. It applies the same principles Robert Camp pioneered at Xerox — and the quality and strategy leaders refined in the decades since — but translates them into a practical, repeatable system accountants can use every day with their clients.

Why this matters for accountants

The history of benchmarking reveals a clear lesson: those who measure themselves against the best learn, adapt, and survive and thrive. Those who don't, fall behind.

Your clients face the same challenge today that Xerox faced in the 1980s. They are competing against stronger, leaner, more innovative businesses. As their accountant, you can either watch them struggle or you can bring the discipline of benchmarking to their table.

This book exists to make that possible.

The science and integrity behind the benchmarks

At TaxFitness, we don't deal in averages, guesswork, or inflated claims. The Top 20% benchmarks are built on a methodology that accountants can rely on with absolute confidence. This isn't theory—it's science, discipline, and integrity combined.

Multiple sources, not one dataset

Our benchmarks are drawn from government data, industry surveys, financial reports, and practitioner feedback. No single dataset is ever enough. We triangulate across multiple sources so the numbers reflect the reality of the market, not a distorted snapshot.

Relevance and recency matter

Old numbers are useless. That's why our weighting system prioritises the most relevant and up-to-date information. Every benchmark reflects current market conditions, not outdated history.

Outliers stripped out

There's always a business at the extreme—either a disaster or a unicorn. Neither tells you what's achievable for your clients. Our process eliminates these outliers, allowing you to work with benchmarks that are realistic, sustainable, and credible.

Segmented and classified properly

Lumping every business into one bucket is lazy. A suburban café isn't the same as a CBD coffee shop. We classify and segment data so your clients can be compared against "like-for-like" operators. That's where true insight comes from.

Cross-checked and reviewed

Every benchmark is validated against market trends and reviewed by industry experts to ensure accuracy and relevance. This step ensures that what you're presenting to clients reflects both the complex data and the lived reality of high performers.

Integrity in how you use it

The benchmarks are a powerful tool—but only when used with integrity. They're not for over-promising or manipulating clients. They're designed to spark conversations, build trust, and create a roadmap for improvement based on evidence.

The result?

A benchmarking system accountants can stand behind. Numbers that are accurate, defensible, and practical. Advice that positions you as the trusted advisor every client wants. That's the science and the integrity behind the Top 20% benchmarks.

About TaxFitness

What is TaxFitness?

TaxFitness is a purpose-built software platform that empowers accountants to deliver high-impact tax planning, Top 20% business benchmarking, and advisory services to their clients. Backed by structured training, marketing resources, and practical support, TaxFitness equips accounting professionals with the tools and confidence to transition from compliance to strategic advisory services.

Imagine presenting your clients with outstanding reports—clear, powerful, and visually compelling—that highlight opportunities for tax savings, profit improvement, asset protection, and wealth creation. With TaxFitness, you're not just lodging returns or preparing financials and BAS; you're helping clients transform their business and investment outcomes.

Using real industry benchmarks, practical strategy databases, and customisable reports, you'll help clients understand how they compare to the top 20% of performers in their industry—and what they need to do to close the gap.

TaxFitness helps you raise the bar and deliver chargeable advisory services that demonstrate value far beyond tax compliance. We provide the systems, tools, and training to help you:

- Create and customise powerful reports
- Explain the insights in clear, strategic language
- Sell the value of the services with confidence
- Price and package advisory services for profitability

Whether you're introducing business benchmarking, expanding your tax planning offerings, or building a recurring advisory revenue stream, TaxFitness gives you the structure and support to deliver.

TaxFitness core functionality:
- Tax planning: Access 250+ ATO-compliant tax strategies, AI-powered recommendations, scenario modelling, and client-ready tax savings reports.
- Top 20% business benchmarking: Benchmark clients

against Top 20% performers in 400+ industries. Instantly identify areas for improvement across key KPIs, including COGS, subcontractors, wages, rent, overheads, and profit margins.

- Business advisory: Choose from 350+ advisory strategies across profit, cash flow, structure, estate planning, succession planning, wealth, and asset protection. Generate visual advisory reports with step-by-step implementation plans.
- AI-powered tools: Includes a strategy engine and chatbot trained on 600+ tax and advisory strategies for fast insights and client advice support.
- Client integration: Import client data directly from Xero, MYOB and QuickBooks. Manage unlimited clients, users, and reports.
- Reporting: Custom-branded reports for tax planning, benchmarking, and business improvement—transparent, visual, and client-focused.
- Marketing, resources & training: Includes brochures, pricing guides, sales scripts, manuals and videos to help you sell and deliver advisory services with confidence.

Who is behind TaxFitness?

TaxFitness is a proudly Australian-owned and operated business, founded in 2017. We operate exclusively from within Australia—no offshore outsourcing, no overseas call centres, and no extended wait times. Our team collaborates to deliver a responsive and high-quality user experience.

All core services—including software, marketing tools, resources, and training programs—are designed specifically for public practice accountants who offer tax planning, benchmarking, and business advisory services.

Our Operations:
- Software development is led by our Melbourne-based partner, Intuitive IT, a trusted Australian development firm.
- Support, demos, and training are delivered directly from our head office located in O'Connor, Western Australia.

At TaxFitness, you're dealing with a local, knowledgeable team that understands the needs of Australian accounting firms—and is committed to helping you deliver high-value, chargeable advisory services with confidence and efficiency.

Meet the team	
  (Founder/CEO) darren.gleeson@ taxfitness.com.au	Darren Gleeson is a leading authority in tax planning and business advisory, with over 20 years of experience in the Australian accounting industry. In 2003, he founded Success Tax Professionals, now Australia's third-largest tax franchise network, with over 75 franchisees lodging more than 50,000 returns annually. In 2017, Darren launched TaxFitness, a tax planning and advisory platform purpose-built for accountants. The software has since expanded to include benchmarking tools and training programs used by 500+ accountants nationwide. Darren holds a Bachelor of Business (Accounting), an MBA, and a Graduate Diploma of Applied Finance. He is a registered Tax Agent, a CPA, and a Graduate Member of the Australian Institute of Company Directors. A prolific author, Darren has written ten books on tax strategy and business performance, including The Tax Planning Advisory System, Tax Planning Made Simple, and Intelligent Accountant. He is passionate about helping accountants move beyond compliance to deliver strategic, high-impact advice that drives client results.

(Founder) tracy.james@ taxfitness.com.au	Together with Darren Gleeson, Tracy James is the founder of Success Tax Professionals, a franchising business that commenced in 2003. Success Tax Professionals offers non-tax agents the opportunity to work towards achieving tax agent status under supervision, while also providing tax agents with mentoring, support, and tools to grow their businesses, offering compliance and higher-tier services. Before joining Success Tax Professionals, Tracy's career history included 20 years of experience in senior management positions in national customer service organisations, including large call centres and government departments, where she was responsible for change management and performance initiatives, such as quality assurance. Tracy has received awards for Project Implementation as well as Learning and Development for several innovative concepts and programmes she created, developed, and rolled out in government workplaces. Tracy's awards include the Australia Day Achievement Award, administered by the National Australia Day Council, and the Australian Training Award (ATA). In TaxFitness, her role focuses on design and information dissemination.
(Director) roydon.snelgar @taxfitness.com. au	Roydon has extensive experience in the industry, with a proven track record of success, having worked in marketing for 15 years and digital marketing for over 10 years. He holds an undergraduate degree in Marketing and a Master of Business Administration from Curtin University of Technology.

How to use this manual in your practice

This manual is designed as both a reference guide and a practical blueprint for accountants who want to deliver Top 20% business benchmarking and advisory services. It shows you not just why benchmarking matters, but exactly how to implement it profitably in your practice.

What the manual covers

The manual explains the TaxFitness Top 20% Business Benchmarking System, a proven 10-step framework that allows accountants to:

- Benchmark client performance against the top 20% of businesses in over 400 industries.
- Translate benchmarking gaps into practical, revenue-generating advisory strategies.
- Build a repeatable, structured service line inside the practice.
- Price, package, and sell benchmarking effectively.
- Manage risk, professional standards, and client expectations.
- Avoid common mistakes and deliver benchmarking consistently year after year.

It also provides background on the history of benchmarking, case studies, practical tools, and future trends so you understand both the discipline and the opportunity.

How to use this manual

- **Read the Introduction first** to understand the purpose, history, and context of benchmarking.
- **Follow the 10 steps in sequence** — each chapter builds on the one before it. Skipping ahead weakens the process.

- **Apply as you go.** Each step includes case studies, checklists, and scripts to guide you through the process. Use these immediately with clients rather than waiting to "finish the book."
- **Train your team.** Assign chapters to staff based on their role, such as data gathering, reporting, and client meetings, and use the manual as an internal training guide.

This is not a book to read once. Please keep it on your desk and refer to it as you implement each step.

Who should use this manual?

This manual is written for:

- **Accounting firm owners and partners** who want to grow advisory revenue and differentiate their practice.
- **Managers and senior accountants** responsible for delivering client-facing benchmarking and advisory services.
- **Practice staff** who play a role in data collection, reporting, and client education.
- **Firms of all sizes** — from sole practitioners to multi-partner firms — that want to move beyond compliance and offer structured, profitable advisory.

Benefits to your practice

By following this system, your practice can expect to:

- **Grow advisory revenue** by introducing a structured service that clients value.
- **Differentiate your firm** — very few accountants currently offer benchmarking, and even fewer do it well.
- **Deepen client relationships** by moving from compliance to a trusted advisor.
- **Build a scalable, repeatable system** — benchmarking

becomes part of your annual service cycle, not an ad hoc project.

- **Protect your practice** by embedding risk management, documentation, and professional standards into advisory.
- **Future-proof your firm** by positioning it around data, strategy, and business improvement.

In summary:
- This manual covers the whole Top 20% benchmarking system — context, process, tools, and future.
- Use it step by step, applying the case studies, checklists, and scripts as you go.
- It is designed for all levels of accounting practice, from owners to staff.
- The benefits are stronger client relationships, higher advisory revenue, and a more competitive practice.

Used this way, the manual is more than a book — it is a working playbook for building and growing a profitable benchmarking division in your firm.

Positioning benchmarking in the accounting profession

Benchmarking isn't new. Consultants, coaches, and banks have been using it for years. But let's be clear: accountants are the only professionals truly positioned to own it.

Why? Accountants sit on the data, understand the numbers, and are trusted with the complete financial story. Everyone else guesses from the outside. Accountants possess the credibility and integrity to transform benchmarking into actionable advice that matters.

And here's the bigger issue: compliance is being commoditised. Software is eating it. Advisory is the future — but "advisory" is too often a buzzword with no substance. Benchmarking changes that. It makes advisory tangible. Structured. Evidence-based. It's the bridge from tax returns to real performance improvement.

For the profession, benchmarking means:

- **Credibility** – advice that's based on fact, not opinion.
- **Differentiation** – owning a space that consultants and banks can't match.
- **Evolution** – a practical path from compliance to advisory.
- **Client demand** – because every business owner wants to know how they compare, and how to improve.

Peter Drucker said it best: "What gets measured gets managed." Benchmarking gives accountants the measurement, and with it, the authority to manage the conversation.

This manual positions benchmarking as more than a service line. It's a **professional obligation**. The accountants who embrace it will be the ones clients turn to first, trust the most, and stay with the longest.

2.

What is the top 20% business benchmarking?

'WHAT GETS MEASURED GETS MANAGED'

– PETER DRUCKER (AUSTRIAN-AMERICAN MANAGEMENT CONSULTANT, AND AUTHOR KNOWN AS THE 'FATHER OF MODERN MANAGEMENT', 1954).

What is top 20% benchmarking?

Top 20% benchmarking is the process of comparing a business's financial performance against the **top-performing 20% of firms** in the same industry, not the average.

It's a method designed to **set the bar higher**, shift the conversation from compliance to improvement, and help clients understand what best-in-class performance looks like.

Why not benchmark against the average?

Most traditional benchmarking tools compare businesses to the mean or median—in other words, the middle of the market. But by definition, the average includes underperforming businesses. That's not the goal.

Your clients don't aspire to be average. They want to be among the best.

Benchmarking against the **top 20%** provides a more meaningful and motivational target. It shows clients:

- What's possible in their industry?

- How far off they are from top-tier performance
- What areas to improve for the most significant financial impact

How the top 20% is defined

The TaxFitness Top 20% Benchmarking System uses a curated database of over 400 industry benchmarks, drawn from ABS, industry data, financial surveys, market reports, historical trend analysis, high-performing private firms, and ATO data.

Each benchmark compares key financial metrics such as:

- Revenue
- Cost of goods sold (COGS)
- Subcontractors
- Rent
- Wages
- Overheads
- Owner's compensation
- Net profit margin

The top 20% values reflect what high-performing businesses in that industry are achieving.

What makes it powerful

This isn't just about comparing numbers. Top 20% benchmarking turns financial data into action by:

- Quantifying underperformance (e.g. "You're paying 8% more in wages than top businesses")
- Framing strategic conversations (e.g. "Here's what's costing you $73,000 per year in margin leakage")
- Providing a roadmap to improve profit, cash flow, and valuation

A gateway to advisory

Top 20% benchmarking doesn't just tell clients where they stand—it opens the door to business improvement, tax planning, pricing changes, staffing reviews, and long-term advisory relationships.

It becomes a trusted reference point for every review meeting, client check-in, and business plan.

It's not just about performance reporting. It's about showing clients what they could achieve—and guiding them to get there.

The origin of the system

The TaxFitness Top 20% Business Benchmarking System was born from a simple frustration: most small business owners work hard, but often without direction, data, or support.

Darren Gleeson, founder of TaxFitness and Success Tax Professionals, has spent over two decades working with small business clients and accountants across Australia. Through that journey, one issue became increasingly clear:

"Small business owners need help to improve performance— but they're not getting it from their current accountant."
— Darren Gleeson

Many firms are still focused solely on compliance. Tax returns are lodged. BAS forms are submitted. But no one is helping business owners understand their numbers, benchmark their performance, or take action to improve.

A passion for business improvement

Darren's passion has always been business improvement. He believes that small businesses—when equipped with the right insights—can grow faster, operate smarter, and become more profitable.

But improvement can't happen without visibility. Without a clear standard, most business owners are operating in the dark.

That's where benchmarking comes into play.

"What gets measured gets managed."
— Peter Drucker

Influenced by the great thinkers

The system draws heavily from the thinking of business improvement pioneers:

"Clarity about what matters provides clarity about what does not."
— Cal Newport

"You can't improve what you don't benchmark."
— W. Edwards Deming

"The message of the Kaizen strategy is that not a day should go by without improvement."
— Masaaki Imai

These principles guided the development of a system that is simple, structured, and focused on real-world outcomes.

Why benchmark the top 20%?

Darren didn't want to build a system that compares businesses to the average. Because average isn't the goal. The benchmark had to be meaningful. It had to set a high standard.

The focus shifted to **the top 20% of businesses in each industry** — those achieving higher profits, better margins, and leaner cost structures. This benchmark provides clients with targets to aspire to, and it offers advisors a clear framework for guidance.

"The top 20% set the standard. Everyone else is just catching up."
— Darren Gleeson

From frustration to framework

What began as a personal frustration has now become a national movement. Over 500 accountants across Australia use the system to deliver actionable benchmarking advice, turning raw financial data into structured improvement strategies.

It's not just a report. It's a conversation starter. A motivator. A roadmap.

And it's changing the way small businesses engage with their advisors.

"Benchmarking transforms financial data into a strategic advantage."
— Darren Gleeson

What makes the system different?

There are many benchmarking tools available, but most fall short in helping accountants deliver real, high-impact advice. They are either too generic, too complex, or too focused on averages that don't inspire change.

The TaxFitness Top 20% Business Benchmarking System was purpose-built for accountants, bookkeepers, BAS agents, and business advisors who want to go beyond compliance and help their clients improve.

Here's what sets it apart:

1. Focus on the top 20% performance, not the average

Most benchmarking tools compare businesses to the mean or

median. This system benchmarks against **the top 20% of firms** in each industry—those with the strongest margins, leanest expenses, and highest net profits. It sets a high-performance standard and shifts your client conversations from average to aspirational.

"Don't show your clients how they compare to the middle of the pack. Show them what the best in their industry are doing."

2. Explicitly built for small business advisors
This is not a corporate finance tool retrofitted for small businesses. It's a system designed for delivering small business advice in meetings, in plain language, and with clear recommendations.

It works whether you're in a small practice, a franchise network, or scaling advisory services within a firm.

3. Covers 400+ industries (and growing)
With industry benchmarks for over 400 business types, the system enables you to deliver relevant, targeted advice to tradespeople, retailers, consultants, professionals, healthcare clinics, manufacturers, and more.

Every benchmark is reviewed and updated to reflect current business realities in Australia.

4. More than numbers — it includes advisory insights
A library of advisory insights and strategy prompts supports each benchmark. These guide you in interpreting the data, asking the right questions, and recommending actions tailored to the client's weaknesses.

You don't just hand over a report—you lead a strategic discussion.

5. Integrated with the TaxFitness platform
The system is fully integrated into the TaxFitness software, so you can:

- Generate benchmarking reports in seconds.
- Tailor them to specific clients or industries.
- Add your comments, recommendations, and branding.
- Include benchmarking inside tax planning, business advisory, or virtual CFO reports.

6. Designed to start and support advisory services
This is not a one-off tool. It's a repeatable system designed to:
- Initiate client advisory conversations
- Support ongoing improvement over time
- Provide a framework for value-based pricing
- Position you as a proactive, strategic advisor

Whether you're launching your advisory offering or expanding it, this system gives you a proven foundation.

In summary: The TaxFitness Top 20% Business Benchmarking System is practical, credible, and designed to help you deliver measurable improvement for your clients—and more revenue for your practice.

It's not just different. It's built for the future of accounting.

Common myths about benchmarking

Despite its value, benchmarking is often misunderstood. Many accountants and business owners avoid it—not because it's ineffective, but because of a few persistent myths. Let's address the most common ones:

Myth 1: "Benchmarking is only for big businesses."
Truth: Benchmarking is more valuable for small and medium businesses, where margins are tighter, time is limited, and decisions are often made without precise data. Knowing how you

compare to the top performers provides clarity and focus, regardless of business size.

Myth 2: "My clients won't be interested in benchmarking."
Truth: In reality, clients are very interested once they understand what it means for their bottom line. Most business owners have never seen how they stack up, and once shown, they're eager to close the gap. Benchmarking helps shift your role from compliance to strategy, and clients value that guidance.

"Benchmarking doesn't bore clients—it wakes them up."

Myth 3: "We already do benchmarking through KPIs."
Truth: KPIs are only meaningful when compared to a standard. Many accountants track client KPIs in isolation, without benchmarking them to top-performing businesses in the same industry. Benchmarking provides context, and without it, KPIs fail to realise their impact fully.

Myth 4: "Benchmarking is too complex to implement."
Truth: With the right system, it's fast, repeatable, and easy to scale. The Top 20% Business Benchmarking System integrates directly into your advisory workflow, generates reports in minutes, and gives you the tools to guide meaningful client conversations—without spreadsheets or complexity.

Myth 5: "It's only useful once a year."
Truth: Benchmarking is not just an annual review tool. It can be used monthly, quarterly, at business check-ins, during tax planning, or when assessing strategy. It's a living advisory tool, not a once-a-year document.

Myth 6: "If my clients are doing OK, there's no need to benchmark."

Truth: Benchmarking isn't just about finding weaknesses—it also highlights untapped opportunities. Even profitable businesses can improve cost control, pricing, or structure. Many clients are doing well, but still leaving thousands on the table.

Final Word: Benchmarking works. It helps businesses improve and helps advisors deliver value.

The key is using a system built specifically for small businesses, backed by real data, and designed to support high-impact conversations, not just reports.

Key definitions and benchmark KPI's

To effectively use the **Top 20% Business Benchmarking System**, it's essential to understand the financial terms and performance indicators that form the foundation of benchmarking. This section defines the key concepts and KPIs used in the system, enabling you to interpret reports accurately, communicate effectively with clients, and deliver actionable advice.

Benchmarking

Benchmarking is the process of comparing a business's financial performance against a peer group or standard. In this system, benchmarks are based on the **top 20% of firms in each industry**, providing your clients with a meaningful, aspirational target, rather than just the average.

Top 20%

Refers to businesses in the **top 20% of financial performance** within a given industry. These businesses have superior cost control, efficient operations, and strong profitability. The system uses its results as the performance benchmark.

Key performance indicators (KPIs)

All financial KPIs are expressed as a percentage of total revenue, allowing consistent comparison between businesses of different sizes.

Core benchmark KPIs (in order of report presentation)

1. Revenue (100%):

Total sales income before any expenses. This is the baseline from which all other KPIs are calculated.

All expenses are expressed as a % of revenue.

2. Cost of goods sold (COGS)

The direct costs of delivering goods or services (e.g., inventory, materials, packaging, freight).

Lower COGS = stronger gross margin.

High COGS may indicate pricing issues, supplier inefficiencies, or inventory mismanagement.

3. Subcontractors

Payments made to contractors, consultants, freelancers, or outsourced providers.

A high subcontractor % may indicate over-reliance on external labour, while a low % could suggest under-utilisation of flexible resourcing.

4. Rent

All expenses related to property leasing, such as commercial premises or retail space.

Rent benchmarks help identify excessive occupancy costs that may be impacting profitability.

5. Wages

Employee salaries and entitlements, excluding payments to the owner. Includes superannuation, allowances, bonuses, and leave provisions.

Excessive wage % may signal overstaffing or inefficiencies. A low wage percentage may indicate under-resourcing or heavy owner involvement.

6. Overheads (Other operating expenses)

General business expenses such as insurance, accounting fees, utilities, office supplies, motor vehicle costs, and advertising.

A high overhead % can erode profit, even when revenue is substantial. Benchmarking helps identify overspending or inefficiencies.

7. Owner's compensation

Total remuneration to the business owner, including wages, drawings, superannuation, dividends, or private expenses paid through the business.

This ensures the business is evaluated after the owner has been paid a commercial wage. Many companies appear profitable only because the owner is underpaid—this KPI corrects that.

8. Net profit (after fair owner's compensation)

The actual profit of the business is **the amount remaining after paying the owner a fair wage for their services**. This figure reflects the actual financial performance of the business.

This is the most important KPI—it shows how well the business is performing after fair owner remuneration. Benchmarking net profit against the top 20% reveals the actual opportunity gap.

Final tip: Benchmarking becomes powerful when you translate %

differences into dollar impact. For example:

"You're spending 4% more on overheads than the top 20%. That's costing you $28,000 per year."

Clear, relatable insights like this turn numbers into decisions—and decisions into results.

How the benchmarks are calculated

The strength of the **Top 20% Business Benchmarking System** lies in its ability to deliver practical, real-world comparisons that accountants and clients can trust. To achieve this, TaxFitness employs a rigorous, proprietary process for sourcing, validating, and calculating benchmarks across more than 400 industries.

1. Sourced from credible, real-world data

The benchmarks are drawn from a wide range of reputable, third-party sources to ensure accuracy and relevance:

a) **Australian Bureau of Statistics (ABS)**
Includes national economic data, industry-level financial metrics, labour cost indexes, and input-output tables.

b) **ASIC company and insolvency data**
Used to identify risk factors and structural financial stress within specific industries.

c) **Industry associations and trade bodies**
Financial summaries and benchmarking reports from national and sector-specific associations (e.g., Franchise Council of Australia, National Retail Association, Master Builders Australia).

d) **Commercial benchmarking and research firms**
Industry insights.

e) **Franchise and buying group reports**
Where available, internal performance data from franchise

networks and buying groups is used to enhance industry-specific accuracy.

f) **Financial surveys and market reports**
National business insights reports (e.g. CommBank Small Business Insights, CPA Australia research, MYOB and Xero trend data) to identify prevailing trends in SME cost structures and profit margins.

g) **Historical trend analysis**
Multi-year data is reviewed to identify and remove anomalies, with a focus on sustainable performance indicators.

h) **ATO small business benchmark data**
Based on tax returns and BAS lodgements, this provides high-integrity financial ratios across a wide variety of small business sectors.

This comprehensive data approach ensures benchmarks reflect real-world business performance, not theoretical models.

2. Standardised financial categories
All financial data is categorised using a consistent structure:
- Revenue
- Cost of Goods Sold (COGS)
- Subcontractors
- Rent
- Wages
- Overheads
- Owner's compensation
- Net profit (after fair owner wage)

These are expressed as a percentage of revenue to ensure consistent comparisons across businesses of all sizes.

3. Focused on the Top 20%

Unlike most tools that benchmark against the average or median, this system isolates the top-performing 20% of businesses in each industry. These are the businesses with:

- Strong net profit margins
- Efficient cost structures
- Sustainable operating models

Benchmarking against the top 20% gives clients an aspirational and actionable performance target.

4. Confidential, proprietary methodology

The process used to compile, adjust, and validate benchmarks is the confidential intellectual property of TaxFitness. It includes:

- Multi-source data triangulation
- Weighting algorithms to reflect relevance and recency
- Outlier removal processes
- Industry segmentation and classification
- Cross-validation against market trends and expert input

This proprietary model is what makes the benchmarking system both credible and commercially robust, trusted by over 500 accountants across Australia.

5. Reviewed and updated regularly

Benchmarks are reviewed annually and updated as needed to reflect:

- Economic and regulatory changes
- Wage and rent fluctuations
- Shifts in business models (e.g., online retail, subcontractor-heavy trades)
- Emerging data from sector-specific research

This ensures the benchmarks remain current, competitive, and relevant to real-world small business conditions.

Important Disclaimer

The benchmarking data provided through this system is general in nature and is intended for comparative and advisory use only. While every effort is made to ensure accuracy, users must exercise professional judgment when interpreting benchmarks and making recommendations.

TaxFitness does not warrant that the data applies to every business circumstance and accepts no liability for any loss arising from decisions made based on benchmarking reports or insights. Users are solely responsible for applying benchmarking information in practice.

Always consider the specific circumstances of each client before providing advice.

3

Why create a top 20% business benchmarking division?

'THE ONLY REAL MISTAKE IS THE ONE FROM WHICH WE LEARN NOTHING'

– HENRY FORD (FOUNDER OF THE FORD MOTOR COMPANY, EARLY 1900S).

Why benchmarking matters

Most business owners make decisions based on instinct, habit, or guesswork, without ever knowing how their performance compares to others in their industry.

That's where benchmarking changes everything.

Benchmarking provides clarity

Benchmarking turns financial data into insight. It allows clients to answer essential questions like:

- Are our costs too high?
- Are we paying staff in line with industry norms?
- Are we making enough profit for the risk and effort involved?

Instead of relying on assumptions or anecdotal comparisons, benchmarking provides objective, data-driven answers. It shows precisely how a business stacks up against the best in the industry—line by line, ratio by ratio.

Top performers benchmark. Average performers don't.
High-performing businesses regularly measure, review, and improve. They know what good looks like and work to close the gap. In contrast, average companies rarely take a step back to assess their performance against external standards.

By introducing benchmarking to your clients, you help them:
- See what's possible
- Understand where they fall short
- Identify where improvement will make the most significant difference
- Take action based on data, not emotion or guesswork

It changes the conversation.
Benchmarking shifts your role from compliance to guidance. It gives you a powerful tool to start strategic conversations:
- "Here's how your business compares to the top 20% of performers in your industry—and here's what that difference means in real dollars."
- It's no longer about explaining financial statements. It's about showing clients how to improve profits, cash flow, and business value—using clear comparisons and practical next steps.

Benchmarking opens the door to advisory.
Benchmarking is the ideal entry point into advisory services. Once clients see where they're underperforming, the next question is:
- "What can we do about it?"

That's where your role as an advisor truly begins—offering strategies, plans, and support to help close the gap and move toward top-tier performance.

In short, benchmarking makes you invaluable.
When you provide benchmarking insights, you become more than just their accountant or bookkeeper—you become their business advisor. You help clients stop flying blind, see the road ahead, and make informed, profitable decisions.

That's why benchmarking matters. And that's why this system exists.

Why clients care about benchmarking

Let me be blunt: business owners don't care about benchmarking reports — they care about results. More profit. Less stress. A business that works.

But here's the kicker — benchmarking is one of the fastest ways to get them there.

I've spent over 20 years in tax and business advisory, and I can tell you this with confidence: clients pay **attention when they realise how far behind they are from where they could be.** That's what benchmarking does. It grabs their attention and makes the invisible visible.

1. It cuts through the noise.
Most clients are running blind. They don't know if their wages are too high, if their rent's killing their profit, or if they're under-charging. They're guessing. Benchmarking stops the guesswork.

When you show a business owner how they compare to the top 20% in their industry, they get it instantly — and they ask, "What do I need to do to fix this?"

Now they're listening. Now they want your advice.

2. It shows them the money
Benchmarking puts real dollars on the table. If your client's net profit is 8% and the industry top 20% is at 20%, that's not just a stat — it's potentially **$120,000+ in lost profit** every year.

Suddenly, the advisory fee isn't an expense — it's an investment. Benchmarking makes the value of advice obvious.

3. It sets a target

Vague goals don't motivate anyone. But show a client that:

"Top operators in your industry are paying 5% less in wages, spending 3% less on rent, and earning double your profit…"

And now they've got a benchmark. A target. Something to aim for. It's no longer about doing better — it's about **closing the gap**.

4. It positions you as the expert

Clients want advisors who understand their industry, not just their accounts. Benchmarking says, "We know what high performance looks like, and we can get you there."

It sets you apart from the accountant down the road who's still just doing tax returns and hoping clients don't ask for more.

5. It leads to action

I've seen it hundreds of times. You show a client the numbers, and they lean in. Their eyes light up. They start asking questions. That's when the real work begins — advisory, implementation, strategy.

Benchmarking isn't just a report. It's a conversation starter. A deal closer. A revenue generator.

Final thought: If you want to shift clients out of compliance mode and into advisory, benchmarking is your foot in the door.

It's not about charts and KPIs — it's about helping your clients build a more profitable, more valuable business.

And when you do that, they stick with you. They refer others. They stop asking what your fees are and start asking what else you can help them with.

That's why clients care about benchmarking.

How benchmarking supports advisory services

In my 20+ years of working with accountants and business owners, one thing has always been clear: clients don't get excited by financial statements. They get excited by results. Benchmarking is the fastest way I know to turn a set of numbers into an "aha" moment that leads to action.

When you compare a client's business to the Top 20% in their industry, you instantly shift the conversation. You're no longer talking about what happened last year—you're showing them what's possible. You're giving them a roadmap to close the gap and move towards elite performance.

Here's why benchmarking is a game-changer for advisory services:

1. It makes the conversation real

When you can point to wages being 8% higher than the Top 20% or COGS being 5% above the benchmark, you're no longer giving vague advice—you're putting hard numbers on the table. That's what makes clients sit up and pay attention.

2. It puts a dollar value on improvement

If you show a client that reducing overheads by 3% will add $40,000 to their bottom line, you're not selling "advisory services"—you're selling them an extra $40,000 a year. That's an easy decision for any business owner.

3. It tells you where to focus first

Businesses always have a long list of things they could improve. Benchmarking makes it clear which changes will deliver the most significant financial wins—and that's where your advisory work starts.

4. It's the foundation for ongoing engagement

One benchmark review is valuable, but quarterly or annual reviews are where the real magic happens. You measure progress, celebrate wins, and find the next opportunity. This is how you build long-term, high-value client relationships.

5. It gives you credibility

These aren't your opinions—they're real industry numbers. When the Top 20% data supports your advice, clients are more likely to trust it, act on it, and pay for it.

6. It sets you apart from other accountants

Most accountants say they offer advisory services. Few can back it up with a structured, evidence-based system that delivers measurable results. Benchmarking is that system—and it's your competitive edge.

Bottom line: Benchmarking serves as the bridge between compliance and true advisory services. It reveals exactly where the profit is hiding, how to access it, and provides the numbers to prove it. Do it right, and you'll transform not just your client's results, but your own practice's profitability.

Ideal implementation roadmap

Implementing the TaxFitness Top 20% Business Benchmarking System doesn't require overhauling your entire practice—it's designed to be implemented progressively and profitably. This roadmap outlines the ideal steps to help you build confidence, build momentum, and build revenue through structured advisory services.

Stage 1: Learn the system (Week 1–2)
Objective: Understand the benchmarking process, tools, and report outputs.
- Firstly, book a TaxFitness demo (if not already done).
- Read this manual from start to finish
- Watch the video training modules in the TaxFitness platform
- Review example reports and templates
- Familiarise yourself with the benchmarks for your core industries

Tip: Start with 2–3 industries you commonly work with (e.g. trades, retail, services)

Stage 2: Trial internally (Week 2–3)
Objective: Build internal confidence by testing the system with known data.
- Benchmark your practice or a friendly client
- Review the benchmarking report internally
- Identify advisory opportunities using the Advisory Insights
- Practice explaining the benchmarks in simple terms

Tip: Use the opportunity to refine how you communicate value to clients.

Stage 3: Pilot with select clients (Week 4–6)
Objective: Deliver your first paid or complimentary benchmarking sessions.
- Choose 3–5 engaged clients for a pilot round
- Run the numbers, prepare reports, and hold benchmarking meetings
- Use the included advisory prompts to guide the discussion

- Ask for feedback and refine your delivery

Tip: Select business clients with whom you already have a strong relationship.

Stage 4: Package & price your service (Week 6–8)
Objective: Turn benchmarking into a formal, priced offering.
- Choose how you will offer benchmarking (one-off, bundled, or ongoing)
- Use the templates in the manual to create pricing and engagement options.
- Update your service menu and onboarding process
- Train your team or admin on data collection and software steps

Tip: Position benchmarking as the gateway to tax planning or business advisory retainers.

Stage 5: Promote to your broader client base (Month 3+)
Objective: Scale your advisory reach.
- Email all eligible business clients with a benchmarking offer.
- Promote through newsletters, review meetings, and webinars
- Share benchmarking case studies and results (with permission)
- Set a goal for the number of benchmarking reports delivered each month

Tip: Use benchmarking reports as the basis for annual business reviews or as a basis for advisory upsells.

Stage 6: Systemise and delegate (Month 4+)
Objective: Make benchmarking a repeatable and team-driven process.

- Document your internal workflow for data entry, report generation, and delivery.
- Delegate report preparation to team members.
- Use scheduling tools and templates to automate client touchpoints
- Consider offering benchmarking in fixed-fee advisory packages

Tip: Use the software's reporting history to track impact and ROI over time.

Long-term outcome
By following this roadmap, you'll establish benchmarking as a high-value, scalable service in your firm—opening doors to strategic advice, deeper client relationships, and recurring advisory revenue.

Case studies – How different-sized practices built benchmarking divisions

Accountants don't want theory — they want proof. These examples illustrate how firms of different sizes established a Top 20% benchmarking division, what they did, and the results achieved. Big or small, the outcome is the same: stronger client relationships, higher advisory revenue, and a real competitive edge.

1. Sole practitioner – Turning compliance into advisory
The practice: One-partner suburban firm with 350 clients. Ninety-five per cent of the work involved straight compliance.

What they did:
- Built benchmarking into annual client tax planning meetings.
- Ran benchmarking reports for 20 key business clients.
- Used the reports as conversation tools to move clients from tax-only to business advisory.

The results:
- Converted 12 clients to advisory packages.
- Added $80,000 in new advisory fees in the first year.
- Locked in stronger retention and picked up four new clients via referrals.

Lesson: Even a sole practitioner can create a benchmarking division by starting with their existing clients. No new marketing, no new systems — just a shift in focus.

2. Small firm (2–3 Partners) – Creating a dedicated business improvement division

The practice: Three-partner firm with 12 staff and 600 SME clients. A good compliance engine, but with flat growth.

What they did:
- Launched a "Business Improvement" division led by one partner.
- Benchmarked 50 clients in the first six months.
- Packaged the service as quarterly benchmarking + strategy sessions.

The results:
- Added $250,000 in recurring advisory fees within 18 months.

- Revenue mix shifted from 90% compliance to 65% compliance / 35% advisory.
- Won new clients specifically because of benchmarking services.

Lesson: Mid-sized firms don't need to reinvent themselves. They need one partner to lead and a system to consistently roll out benchmarking.

3. Mid-tier firm – Embedding benchmarking across the practice
The practice: Eight partners, 60 staff. Compliance-heavy but ambitious to grow advisory.

What they did:
- Integrated benchmarking into compliance workflow for 40% of SME clients.
- Trained managers to deliver benchmarking meetings with a standardised playbook.
- Used benchmarking reports and case studies in marketing to win new clients.

The results:
- Advisory revenue doubled in two years.
- Average fee per client increased 30%.
- Firm built a reputation as the region's leader in business improvement.

Lesson: At scale, benchmarking is most effective when integrated into workflows. Train the team, make it routine, and advisory becomes part of every client relationship.

Key takeaway: It doesn't matter if you're a one-partner suburban practice or a 60-staff mid-tier firm. Benchmarking divisions work. The practices that lead with benchmarking win more clients, generate recurring advisory revenue, and solidify their role as trusted advisors. The only difference between firms that do and firms that don't is who decides to start.

The business case for creating a benchmarking division

To grow your practice, retain clients longer, and differentiate yourself from the competition, it's essential to move beyond relying solely on compliance work. Compliance pays the bills — but benchmarking and advisory work build the business.

Creating a Top 20% Business Benchmarking Division is one of the easiest and fastest ways to add high-value advisory services to your firm. It's not complicated, it's not risky, and the payoff can be huge.

1. It pays for itself fast

The average firm that introduces benchmarking to its top business clients adds $30,000 to $100,000 in new fees in the first year. No extra staff, no significant overhead increase — just a more intelligent conversation with clients that leads straight into advisory work.

2. Double your client value

Once you start benchmarking, you'll uncover tax planning opportunities, profit improvement strategies, and growth plans your clients never knew existed. For many firms, this doubles the revenue from a single client compared to compliance-only work.

3. Clients love it

Business owners don't get excited about last year's financials —

they want to know how to make next year better. Benchmarking shows them:

- Where they rank against the best in their industry.
- Where the profit leaks are hiding
- Which changes will give them the fastest return

When you can give those answers with hard numbers, they'll listen — and they'll act.

4. No new licences or red tape

You already have the base skills from your compliance work. Adding benchmarking doesn't require new licences or extra registrations — just a system that turns your knowledge into measurable client results.

5. The opportunity is huge

Approximately 80% of business clients can increase their profits with the right strategies. Benchmarking provides you with the evidence and numbers to make those conversations easy.

6. It puts you ahead of competitors

Most accountants talk about advisory. Very few can back it up with a structured, evidence-based process. A benchmarking division instantly sets you apart.

7. Referrals take off

Deliver measurable improvements, and your clients will speak highly of you. You'll get more referrals, better-quality clients, and you'll spend less time chasing work.

Bottom line: A Top 20% Business Benchmarking Division isn't just another service line — it's a growth engine. It drives higher fees, stronger client relationships, and makes you the accountant business owners want to work with.

Case study – How benchmarking transformed a client and a practice

Implementing industry: Building & construction
Original service level: Annual compliance – $3,000/year

Background

Two years ago, a mid-sized accounting firm was providing basic compliance work for a building industry client. The business was generating $12 million annually, but despite its size, profitability was low.

Two working directors were taking home only $300,000 combined in profit. The accountant knew something was wrong, but without complex comparative data, the conversation around "how to improve" wasn't getting traction.

Benchmarking reveals the gap

The accountant introduced the Top 20% Business Benchmarking System.

The first benchmarking review showed:

- Subcontractor costs were 70% of revenue, far above the Top 20% benchmark of 40% for similar building firms.
- Profit margins were well below industry leaders.

Cash flow was tight despite high revenue. By presenting the findings in clear, line-by-line comparisons, the client could see exactly where they were bleeding money and how much profit was being left on the table.

The advisory process

The client moved to quarterly benchmarking reviews, each one followed by specific action plans:

- Renegotiating subcontractor rates and contracts.
- Bringing some work in-house to reduce reliance on high-cost subcontractors.
- Tightening project management to reduce cost overruns
- Improving scheduling and resource allocation to boost productivity

The results

After 12 months:

- Profit increased from $300,000 to $756,000.
- Subcontractor costs dropped significantly, closing much of the gap to the Top 20% benchmark.
- Directors had more confidence in pricing and project control

After 24 months:

- Profit reached close to $2 million
- The business had entirely restructured its cost base, creating a much more sustainable and profitable model
- The directors had shifted from "working in the business" to focusing on strategic growth

The win for the accountant

Benchmarking turned a $3,000/year compliance client into a $48,000/year advisory client. The accountant now charges $4,000 per month for ongoing benchmarking and strategic support — and the client views it as a bargain due to the clear return on investment.

Key lessons

- Benchmarking creates urgency — the client saw the numbers and wanted to act immediately.
- Regular reviews keep the momentum — quarterly check-ins ensured continuous improvement.
- Advisory fees are easy to justify when you can show a direct link between your advice and their profit growth.

Bottom line: This case demonstrates the transformative power of benchmarking, benefiting both the client's business and the accountant's revenue stream. One benchmarking conversation evolved into a $ 48,000-per-year advisory relationship — and resulted in an additional $1.7 million in annual profit for the client.

4.
TaxFitness Top 20% business benchmarking system

'MEASUREMENT IS THE FIRST STEP THAT LEAD TO CONTROL AND EVENTUALLY TO IMPROVEMENT'

– H. JAMES HARRINGTON (AMERICAN ENGINEER AND QUALITY MANAGEMENT EXPERT KNOWN FOR BUSINESS PROCESS IMPROVEMENT, 1990S)

Flow chart of the 10-step top 20% business benchmarking system

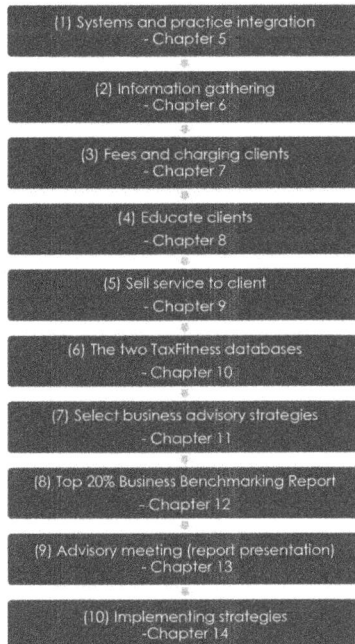

(1) Systems and practice integration - Chapter 5

(2) Information gathering - Chapter 6

(3) Fees and charging clients - Chapter 7

(4) Educate clients - Chapter 8

(5) Sell service to client - Chapter 9

(6) The two TaxFitness databases - Chapter 10

(7) Select business advisory strategies - Chapter 11

(8) Top 20% Business Benchmarking Report - Chapter 12

(9) Advisory meeting (report presentation) - Chapter 13

(10) Implementing strategies -Chapter 14

Step 1 - Systems and practice integration

'SUCCESS IS NOT THE KEY TO HAPPINESS. HAPPINESS IS THE KEY TO SUCCESS'

– ALBERT SCHWEITZER (ALSATIAN, THEOLOGIAN, MUSICIAN, AND MEDICAL MISSIONARY. NOBEL PEACE PRIZE WINNER, 1950S)

You are at STEP 1

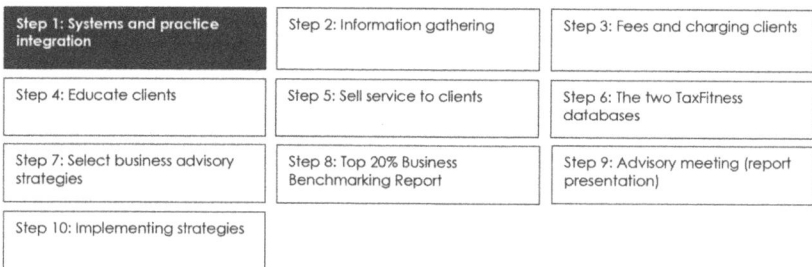

Step 1: Systems and practice integration	Step 2: Information gathering	Step 3: Fees and charging clients
Step 4: Educate clients	Step 5: Sell service to clients	Step 6: The two TaxFitness databases
Step 7: Select business advisory strategies	Step 8: Top 20% Business Benchmarking Report	Step 9: Advisory meeting (report presentation)
Step 10: Implementing strategies		

Why systems matter for benchmarking

I've been in this industry long enough to know one thing — without systems, nothing scales. You can have the best benchmarking data in the world, but if it's delivered inconsistently, late, or in a way that's different every time, it won't stick.

Top 20% benchmarking is not something you "try" on a client here and there. It's a structured, repeatable process. If you get the systems right, it runs like clockwork. If you don't, it becomes a time-draining distraction that dies after a few months.

Here's why systems matter:

1. Consistency drives credibility

Clients trust what's consistent. Every benchmarking report should have the same level of accuracy, professionalism, and visual impact, no matter who in the firm delivers it.

2. Speed equals perceived value

If it takes you three weeks to deliver a benchmarking report, the momentum is gone. A system enables you to transition from client data to a completed report in hours, not weeks.

3. No reinventing the wheel

Without systems, every job feels like starting from scratch. With systems, you follow a proven process that works the same way every time.

4. Scalability without chaos

A system means you can deliver benchmarking to 20, 50, or 100 clients a year without blowing up your workflow.

5. Easier to train staff

A well-documented system means anyone in your team can follow the process and deliver a high-quality result, not just you.

The goal is simple: Please set up your benchmarking process so it's as predictable and repeatable as compliance. If compliance can run like a machine, so can benchmarking. The difference? Compliance keeps the lights on. Benchmarking grows the business — yours and your clients.'

Objectives of systems

Systems aren't paperwork. Systems aren't bureaucracy. Systems are the blueprint that takes a great idea — like Top 20% benchmarking — and turns it into a reliable, profitable service that runs without you having to personally push it along every time.

When you strip it back, the objectives of your benchmarking system are simple:

1. Standardise delivery

Every client receives the same process, quality, and level of professionalism. That's how you build trust and a reputation for excellence.

2. Ensure accuracy

Benchmarking is data-driven. A small mistake in numbers can lead to big mistakes in advice. A system catches errors before they reach the client.

3. Increase efficiency

Time is your most valuable resource. A well-built system enables you to deliver more benchmarking reports in less time, without compromising quality.

4. Create a consistent client experience

Clients should feel like they're working with a well-oiled machine, not a "wing it" service. Consistency builds confidence, and confidence leads to more advisory work.

5. Make the service scalable

Without systems, you're capped at how much you can deliver. With systems, you can roll benchmarking out to dozens — even hundreds — of clients without adding stress or chaos.

The test is this: if you went on holiday tomorrow, could someone else in your team follow your system and deliver a benchmarking report exactly the way you would? If the answer's no, you don't have a system yet — you have a habit. And habits don't scale.

The objective of practice integration

Having a benchmarking system is one thing. Embedding it into your practice so it runs automatically is another.

Practice integration means Top 20% benchmarking isn't something you offer if the client asks for it — it's something you deliver because it's part of how your firm operates.

The objectives here are clear:

1. Make benchmarking a core service, not an optional extra

If you treat benchmarking as a side project, clients will likely do the same. It should be integrated into your advisory process as a standard for every qualifying business client.

2. Embed benchmarking in the client lifecycle

- New client onboarding? Include a benchmarking report.
- Annual review? Update their benchmarks.
- Quarterly meeting? Compare their performance and set targets.

It's not an event — it's an ongoing conversation.

3. Create predictable, recurring revenue

Integration means you're not chasing one-off jobs. You're locking in ongoing benchmarking fees as part of a broader advisory service. That's how you stabilise and grow cash flow.

4. Link benchmarking to action and accountability

A benchmarking report without follow-up is just an expensive PDF. Integration involves reviewing results, agreeing on action steps, and tracking progress.

5. Make it part of the culture

Your team should view benchmarking in the same way they view compliance — as a standard practice the firm follows. No exceptions. No debate.

The reality is this: If benchmarking sits "off to the side" of your primary practice processes, it will fade away the moment you get busy. If it's baked into your systems and culture, it will run — and make money — every week of the year.

Technology integration

Technology is the backbone of delivering a consistent, efficient, and profitable benchmarking service. Without the right systems talking to each other, benchmarking becomes a manual, time-consuming process that's prone to errors. When technology is integrated well, you create a seamless flow of information — from the client's accounting software to your analysis tools, reporting templates, and client communication platforms.

For Top 20% benchmarking, technology integration isn't just about convenience. It's about:

- Accuracy: Minimising human error in data entry and transfer.
- Speed: Reducing turnaround time from weeks to days — or even hours.
- Scalability: Allowing your firm to deliver benchmarking to dozens or hundreds of clients without additional strain on your team.

1. Core technology stack

At the heart of your benchmarking service is a set of interconnected tools. For most firms, this includes:

a) Accounting platforms
- Client data comes directly from systems like Xero, MYOB, QuickBooks, or other cloud platforms.
- Bank feeds, invoices, payroll, and expenses are already reconciled, providing clean, up-to-date data.

b) TaxFitness benchmarking software
- Imports raw client financials.
- Automatically calculates industry KPIs and compares them to Top 20% benchmarks.
- Generates advisory insights tailored to performance gaps.
- Client-ready benchmarking reports including automatically populated graphs, charts, and commentary. Exportable to Word and PDF.

c) CRM and practice management
- Platforms like Karbon, FYI Docs, or WorkflowMax ensure each benchmarking project is tracked, assigned, and delivered on time.

d) Client communication platforms
- Zoom, Microsoft Teams, or in-office presentations for delivering reports and action plans.
- Secure portals for document sharing and report storage.

2. Integration best practices
To get the most from your technology:

a) Automate data flow
- Use direct API connections where possible to pull financial data into TaxFitness without manual downloading or CSV uploads.
- Avoid re-keying figures — every manual entry is an opportunity for mistakes.

b) Standardise file structures
- Use consistent naming conventions for files and folders (e.g., ClientName_YYYY_Benchmarking.pdf).
- Store benchmarking files in a dedicated folder structure within your document management system.

c) Synchronise calendars and tasks
- Link your practice management system to your email and calendar so that client meetings, follow-ups, and report deadlines are automatically scheduled.

d) Secure client data
- Implement two-factor authentication for all cloud platforms.
- Use encryption and secure portals to protect sensitive client financials.

3. Building for the future
Technology in accounting is evolving rapidly. Firms that build integration into their benchmarking service now will:
- Be ready for AI-powered forecasting and predictive analytics.

- Reduce administrative time by up to 50% through automation.
- Deliver a client experience that feels modern, responsive, and data-driven.

Practice tip: Every extra click in your process is wasted time. Map your current benchmarking tech workflow and remove any steps that could be automated or eliminated. The goal is to have one source of truth for client data and to minimise the time between receiving the data and delivering value to the client.

Australian business benchmarking options

Selecting the right benchmarking software is a critical step in embedding Top 20% business benchmarking into your practice systems. The Australian market offers a range of tools, each with different capabilities, data sources, and integration options. Understanding the landscape will help you select the platform that best fits your advisory goals.

1. Dedicated benchmarking platforms

Purpose-built solutions are specifically designed to compare client performance against industry benchmarks.

- Pros: Largest benchmark databases, tailored reporting, purpose-built for advisory services.
- Cons: Limited functionality outside benchmarking.

2. Business advisory suites with benchmarking modules

Advisory platforms that include benchmarking as one of many features.

- Pros: Broader advisory tools (cash flow, valuations, scenario modelling).
- Cons: Benchmark databases may be smaller or based on overseas data, reducing Australian relevance.

3. DIY spreadsheet-based solutions

Custom-built Excel or Google Sheets templates using publicly available data.

- Pros: Low cost, complete control over formulas and presentation.
- Cons: Time-consuming to maintain, higher risk of errors, limited to the skill and data available to the preparer.

4. Industry-specific benchmarking tools

Platforms designed for one sector (e.g., retail, hospitality, trades).

- Pros: Highly relevant to that industry, with deep operational KPIs.
- Cons: Not suitable for firms serving a broad client base.

Key criteria when selecting benchmarking software

When evaluating options, consider:

a) Australian data sources: Benchmarks must be based on Australian businesses for local accuracy.

b) Industry coverage: The number of industries and niche sectors covered.

c) Data recency: Frequency of updates and alignment with current market conditions.

d) Integration: Ability to connect with accounting systems (e.g., Xero, MYOB, QuickBooks).

e) Reporting quality: Client-friendly, professional reports that support advisory conversations.

f) Advisory support: Additional tools, insights, and training to help you turn data into actionable advice.

Software & Website	Year Founded	Primary Focus	Australian Data Sources	Industry Coverage	Benchmarking Depth
MAUS Business Systems www.maus.com.au	1990	Business planning, KPIs & advisory tools	Partial AU data	Broad – general business sectors	Medium – KPIs vary by module
Benchmarking.com.au www.benchmarking.com.au	1994	Benchmark data & comparison reports for accountants	100% Australian	~100 industries	Medium – primarily financial KPIs
Bstar www.bstar.com.au	2001	Advisory framework with benchmarking & practice development tools	100% Australian	Broad – common industries	Medium – general KPI sets
Calxa www.calxa.com	2008	Budgeting & cash flow forecasting with basic benchmarking	Limited AU data	Broad – general industries	Low – high-level financial KPIs
Spotlight Reporting www.spotlightreporting.com	2011	Forecasting & reporting suite with benchmarking	Mostly global, some AU	Broad – general industries	Medium – financial KPIs only
Fathom www.fathomhq.com	2012	Financial analysis & reporting with benchmarking module	Mostly global, some AU	Broad – common industries only	Medium – limited to selected metrics
TaxFitness www.taxfitness.com.au	2017	Dedicated Australian Top 20% benchmarking & advisory for accountants	100% Australian	400+ industries, including niche sectors	High – full KPI sets for Top 20%
DIY Spreadsheets N/A	N/A	Custom-built by a firm	Depends on the source	Unlimited if data is available	Variable – depends on data & design

Benchmarking quality control

Benchmarking is only as good as the data and process behind it. You can have the most advanced benchmarking platform in the world, but if your inputs are wrong, your outputs will be incorrect. And when that happens, the credibility of your advisory work takes a hit.

Quality control is about building confidence in your clients and your team that every benchmarking report you produce is accurate, consistent, and reliable.

Why quality control matters

When you present benchmarking results, you're positioning yourself as the authority. Clients will make decisions — sometimes big ones — based on those numbers. That means you need to ensure your figures align. A single error can damage trust and undo months of relationship building.

Core principles of benchmarking quality control

1. **Data accuracy comes first**
    - Verify all financial and KPI inputs before running reports.
    - Cross-check figures against source documents, not just client-supplied summaries.

2. **Consistency across clients**
    - Use the same KPI definitions, timeframes, and calculation methods for all engagements.
    - Inconsistent methods lead to inconsistent advice, and that leads to client confusion.

3. **Industry benchmark integrity**
    - Ensure the benchmark data is current and relevant to the client's actual industry.
    - Avoid using "near enough" matches just to get a report out quickly.

4. **Report review process**
    - A second set of eyes should review every benchmarking report before it's presented to the client.
    - This isn't about mistrusting your team — it's about building in a safeguard for your reputation.

5. **Documentation & audit trail**
    - Keep a clear record of the source data, the date of the report, and any adjustments made.
    - This protects you if a client ever questions the numbers months down the track.

Embedding quality control in your firm
- Checklists: Use a pre-report checklist to confirm all data points have been validated.
- Standard operating procedures (SOPs): Document the exact steps for preparing, reviewing, and approving benchmarking reports.
- Training: Make sure all staff understand the importance of accuracy and the firm's quality control processes.
- Technology: Use your benchmarking platform's built-in data validation tools where available.

Key perspective:
"When I hand a client a benchmarking report, I want to know — not hope—that every number is rock-solid. The moment you present a wrong figure, you lose a little bit of trust. Do that twice, and you lose the client. Quality control isn't red tape; it's the insurance policy for your reputation."

Automation and reporting efficiency

One of the most significant barriers to delivering benchmarking at scale is the time it takes to collect data, prepare reports, and present results. If your process relies heavily on manual work, you'll either:
1. Avoid offering benchmarking altogether because it's too time-consuming, or
2. Deliver it sporadically when you "find the time", which means you never really scale.

Automation changes that. When you integrate your benchmarking platform into your practice systems and use its automation features effectively, benchmarking becomes fast, consistent, and profitable.

Why Automation Matters

- Time savings: Less time spent on data entry means more time for advisory conversations.
- Consistency: Automated processes reduce the risk of human error and ensure every report follows the same standard.
- Scalability: When the process is quick, you can offer benchmarking to more clients without adding extra staff.

Core areas for automation

1. Data import & integration

- Connect your benchmarking platform to your accounting software (e.g., Xero, MYOB, QuickBooks) to pull in financial data automatically.
- Use mapping templates to ensure each account maps to the correct KPI category.

2. Report generation

- Use your benchmarking platform's pre-set templates for consistent report layouts.
- Customise templates once, then apply them across all clients.

3. Recurring reporting schedules

- Set up automatic reminders to run quarterly or annual benchmarking reports.
- Schedule the report generation so it's ready before client review meetings.

4. Visualisation & charts

- Leverage built-in visual reporting tools for instant graphs, comparisons, and KPI dashboards.

- Avoid recreating charts in Excel — use the platform's native design tools.

Reporting efficiency tips
- Batch processing: Run multiple client reports at the same time to save setup and processing time.
- Pre-meeting preparation: Automate the delivery of draft reports to your inbox for review before the client meeting.
- Reusable commentary: Build a library of commentary and insights linked to common KPI variances, so you can drop them into reports without starting from scratch.
- Client-friendly formats: Deliver reports in a format that's easy for clients to read (PDF or presentation), rather than raw data tables.

Key perspective:
"If you're spending more than 30 minutes preparing a benchmarking report, you're doing it wrong. The goal is simple: have the system do the heavy lifting so you can focus on explaining the numbers and giving advice — the part clients value and will pay for."

Staff training & change management

You can have the best benchmarking system in the country, but if your team doesn't know how to use it — or doesn't want to — it's going to sit idle. The success of Top 20% benchmarking in your firm depends on two things:
1. Staff capability – knowing precisely what to do.
2. Staff buy-in – wanting to do it.

Training gives them the capability. Change management gives them the buy-in.

Why staff training is essential

Benchmarking is different from compliance work. It's not just plugging numbers into a form — it's about interpreting data, spotting opportunities, and having valuable conversations with clients.

That means your team needs to be trained in:

- The firm's benchmarking workflow (from data gathering to report delivery).
- Using the benchmarking platform efficiently.
- Understanding KPIs and how they link to business performance.
- Communicating benchmarking results in plain English to clients.

Key elements of a training program

1. Initial training for all relevant staff

- Walk through the end-to-end process using a real client example.
- Include both the technical (software, data entry, report generation) and the advisory (what the numbers mean) aspects.

2. Role-specific focus

- Accountants & analysts: Input accuracy, KPI calculations, and interpreting results.
- Client managers & advisors: Explaining results, linking findings to advisory recommendations, managing client expectations.
- Admin & support: Scheduling, report formatting, and follow-up processes.

3. Ongoing refresher training
- Short quarterly sessions to reinforce best practices, share tips, and review any updates to benchmarks or software features.

4. New hire induction
- Benchmarking training should be part of your onboarding for any new team member who will touch the process.

Change management – getting staff buy-in

Introducing benchmarking can be a significant shift for some firms. It's not "just another report" — it's a service that requires a different mindset. To get staff on board:

1. Communicate the why – Explain how benchmarking benefits clients, improves the firm's reputation, and creates new revenue streams.
2. Involve staff early – Let them help shape workflows, checklists, and client presentation formats.
3. Show quick wins – Start with a small set of clients and share the results with the team. Seeing a client respond positively builds momentum.
4. Address concerns openly – Some staff may feel uncertain about advisory work. Offer support, mentoring, and script examples for client conversations.

Darren's perspective:

"The number one reason a new service fails in an accounting firm isn't the software — it's the people. Train them well, involve them in the process, and show them early wins. Once they see clients' eyes light up when they understand their numbers, you'll have a team that's fully invested."

Ongoing monitoring & refinement

Benchmarking is not a "set and forget" service. Once it's in place, you need structured monitoring to keep it accurate, consistent, and profitable. This is how you maintain quality and ensure the service continues to deliver results for clients and the firm.

System monitoring framework

1. Data currency
- Confirm the benchmarking platform is using the latest industry data.
- Update advisory talking points when benchmarks shift.

2. Report accuracy & consistency
- Conduct random spot checks on completed reports.
- Verify KPI calculations and confirm the industry match is correct.

3. Client uptake & outcomes
- Track the number of clients benchmarked each quarter.
- Measure business improvements following the implementation of recommendations.

4. Workflow efficiency
- Monitor turnaround time from data collection to report delivery.
- Identify and remove recurring bottlenecks.

5. Team capability
- Observe client meetings to ensure results are explained clearly and linked to strategies.
- Provide refresher training where gaps are identified.

Continuous refinement actions
- Quarterly process review: Assess accuracy, efficiency, and client feedback as a team.
- Technology optimisation: Apply new platform features and integrations to save time and improve output.
- Industry coverage expansion: Add benchmarks for emerging client sectors.
- Report enhancement: Keep reports visually engaging and simple for clients to understand.

Case study – systems in action (Sole practitioner)

Background
A sole practitioner operating from a home office wanted to expand into advisory services without increasing working hours or hiring staff. Compliance work covered the bills, but there was little time left for higher-value client conversations.

Step 1 – Choosing the platform
The practitioner selected TaxFitness for its automation, 400+ Australian industry benchmarks, and AI-generated advisory insights. The goal was to deliver benchmarking as a premium add-on to existing business clients, without increasing admin workload.

Step 2 – Workflow integration
The benchmarking process was streamlined into a simple, repeatable routine:
- Data import from Xero, MYOB and QuickBooks into Tax-Fitness.
- Automatic KPI calculation and industry benchmark selection.
- Quick review for accuracy using the quality control checklist.

- Report generation in a standard firm-branded template.
- Presentation during quarterly or annual review meetings (in-person or via Zoom).

With automation, complete benchmarking reports were prepared in under 15 minutes.

Step 3 – Client rollout

The practitioner began with a small pilot, involving five clients across different industries, and quickly received positive feedback. The service was then offered to all business clients, bundled with an annual review meeting.

Step 4 – Results after 12 months

- Client uptake: 50% of business clients now receive benchmarking reports.
- Advisory revenue: Increased by $40,000 annually.
- Time efficiency: All benchmarking delivered within regular working hours, no extra admin staff required.
- Client outcomes: One café client reduced wastage by 4% and increased net profit by $22,000 after implementing recommendations.

Lessons learned

- Even without staff, benchmarking can be scaled using automation and a transparent workflow.
- Bundling benchmarking with annual reviews created a natural entry point for advisory conversations.
- Early client wins built confidence and word-of-mouth referrals.

Case study – systems in action (Two partners and ten staff)

Background

A suburban accounting firm with two partners and 10 staff members wanted to grow its advisory revenue without increasing compliance work. They decided to roll out Top 20% business benchmarking across their business client base.

Before implementation, benchmarking was sporadic. Reports were prepared manually in Excel, taking hours per client, and were used with only a small number of clients each year.

Step 1 – Choosing the platform

The partners selected **TaxFitness** for its 400+ Australian industry benchmarks, Xero integration, and AI-generated advisory insights. They committed to making benchmarking part of their standard review process.

Step 2 – Workflow integration

The firm built benchmarking into its practice management system:

- Data import from Xero, MYOB and QuickBooks into Tax-Fitness.
- Automatic KPI calculation and industry benchmark matching.
- Quality control check by a senior accountant.
- Report generation using a customised firm template.
- Delivery in quarterly or annual client review meetings.

Automation cut report prep time from two hours to under 20 minutes.

Step 3 – Staff training & change management

- All team members received role-specific training:

- Accountants learned data mapping, imports, and report generation.
- Advisors practised presenting results in plain English and linking KPIs to strategies.
- A one-month pilot with 10 clients helped refine the process before full rollout.

Step 4 – Quality control & ongoing monitoring
A quality control checklist was built into the workflow. Spot checks were done quarterly to ensure accuracy in KPI calculations and correct industry selection.

Step 5 – Results after 12 Months
- Client uptake: 60% of business clients now receive benchmarking reports.
- Advisory revenue: Increased by $120,000 annually, with many clients paying for quarterly reviews.
- Time saved: Over 120 staff hours freed up annually through automation.
- Client outcomes: One trades client reduced overheads by 5% and increased net profit by $68,000 after acting on recommendations.

Lessons learned
- Embedding benchmarking into the systems made it sustainable.
- Automation freed time for advisory work, not admin.
- Quality control ensured reports were accurate and credible.
- Staff buy-in came from early wins and a simple, repeatable process.

6

Step 2 – Information gathering

'IF YOU CAN'T MEASURE IT, YOU CAN'T CHANGE IT'

– PETER DRUCKER, (MANAGEMENT CONSULTANT, 1960S)

You are at STEP 2

Step 1: Systems and practice	**Step 2: Information gathering**	Step 3: Fees and charging clients
Step 4: Educate clients	Step 5: Sell service to clients	Step 6: The two TaxFitness databases
Step 7: Select business advisory strategies	Step 8: Top 20% Business Benchmarking Report	Step 9: Advisory meeting (report presentation)
Step 10: Implementing strategies		

Purpose of information gathering

If you start with the wrong information, you'll end with bad advice. It's that simple.

The role of this step is to collect accurate, complete, and relevant information, ensuring your benchmarking work stands on solid ground. This isn't a tick-the-box exercise. It's a targeted process designed to give you a crystal-clear picture of the client's business and personal situation, so you can compare it to the Top 20% and identify the fastest, safest ways to improve performance.

Every question you ask needs a reason. You're not here to waste the client's time, and you're not here to fill out a form for the sake of it. You're here to uncover facts that will directly shape your analysis and recommendations.

The purpose is fourfold:

1. Get the actual financial position. Look beyond the P&L — understand cash flow, debt, assets, and the bigger financial picture.
2. Clarify what matters most to the client. Their goals and priorities will guide where you focus your improvement strategies.
3. Spot the gaps and strengths. Identify where they're under-performing against the Top 20% and where they already have an advantage.
4. Build trust. Demonstrate to the client that you're thorough, professional, and committed to finding the best solutions for them.

Benchmarking is all about evidence. Without the correct data, you're guessing — and clients don't pay for guesses. With the correct data, you can:

- Pinpoint exactly where the business is leaking profit.
- Quantify the upside in dollars.
- Recommend strategies that are clear, measurable, and achievable.

The bottom line:

- Get the facts right, and the advice writes itself.
- Get the facts wrong, and nothing else in the process will work.

When you gather the correct information, you set up every other step in the Top 20% Business Benchmarking System for success.

Understanding the client's current financial position

If you don't understand your client, you can't give them advice that matters. It's that simple.

One of the main reasons accountants fail to get traction with benchmarking services is that they only have part of the picture. They've seen last year's accounts or a few key numbers, but they don't have a clear view of the whole business and personal situation.

When you don't know the client's **current position** and you don't know **what they want to achieve**, you're guessing. You risk delivering insights that don't hit the mark, and the client tunes out, not because benchmarking isn't valuable, but because it doesn't feel relevant to them.

If you want clients to act on your benchmarking recommendations, you need the whole picture. That's where the **Interview Checklist** comes in.

The checklist keeps the process tight and consistent. It ensures that you collect the correct information in the right order every time. By doing this, you establish an accurate baseline of where the client is today, allowing you to show them exactly how far they are from the Top 20% and what needs to change.

Information to be collected:

Client	Spouse	Entity 1
• Goals (short-term and long-term). • Children, parents and dependents. • Assets (includes business value). • Liabilities • Income • Expenses	• Goals (short-term and long-term) • Children, parents and dependents. • Assets (includes business value). • Liabilities • Income • Expenses	(if applicable, compile for each entity) • Goals (short-term and long-term) • Directors, trustees, shareholders and beneficiaries • Assets • Liabilities • Income • Expenses

When you have this information, you can:

- See the client's real financial position — not just a P&L snapshot.
- Identify where they're underperforming compared to the Top 20% in their industry.
- Quantify the improvement gap in dollars and percentages.
- Link your recommendations directly to the client's goals so they're motivated to act.

Key point: You can't benchmark a business properly if you don't know where it's starting from. The Interview Checklist makes sure you do.

Understanding what is essential to the client

If you don't know what matters to a client, you can't give them advice that matters. Simple as that.

Every client is different. Two businesses in the same industry, with the same turnover, can have completely different priorities. One wants to double sales and take on the world. The other wants to cut hours, reduce stress, and have a life outside the business.

Until you know this client's priorities — their wants, their aspirations — you're flying blind. And when you're flying blind, you guess. When you guess, you miss.

That's why Step 2 of the Top 20% Business Benchmarking process isn't just about the numbers. It's about understanding what the client wants to achieve, both in their business and in their personal life.

The **Interview Checklist** makes this easy. It forces the conversation. It uncovers the 13 most common client wants and puts them on the table, allowing you to focus your benchmarking analysis where it will have the most significant impact.

The 13 client wants (Aspirations);

1. Minimise tax now and in the future – legally and sustainably.
2. Increase profit – and by how much? The number matters.
3. Grow sales – expand the revenue base.
4. Protect assets from creditors, lawsuits, or divorce.
5. Increase cash flow – smooth it, strengthen it.
6. Work less, reduce stress, improve lifestyle – make the business work for the owner, not the other way around.
7. Increase wealth – and set a dollar target.
8. Security and peace of mind – financial stability and confidence.
9. Estate planning – looking after loved ones.
10. Succession planning – have a plan
11. Selling the business – have a plan for the exit.
12. Work as an owner, not as a technician – run the business, don't just work in it.
13. Achieve personal goals – define them clearly.
14. Finance readiness – building financial health to get the right loan on good terms.

When you know these wants, you can:
- Make your benchmarking analysis relevant to the client sitting in front of you.
- Link performance gaps directly to outcomes they care about.
- Show them the financial path to achieving their goals.

Key point: Benchmarking that's not connected to the client's priorities is just a spreadsheet. Connect it, and it becomes a blueprint for action.

Types of information required

If you want to benchmark a business against the Top 20%, you can't work off half-baked numbers and vague guesses. You need accurate, complete, and relevant information — the kind of data that tells you exactly where the client is starting from and where the opportunities lie.

This isn't about drowning the client in forms or collecting every scrap of paper they've got. It's about gathering the correct information — the stuff that will feed into the benchmarking analysis and give you insights you can turn into action.

There are three broad categories of information you need:

1. Financial position

This is the complex data. Without it, you're operating in the dark. You need to know:

- Revenue,
- Cost of goods sold.
- Subcontractor costs.
- Wages
- Rent,
- Overheads,
- Owner's compensation.
- Net profit before tax.
- Assets and liabilities — including the value of the business itself.

This financial snapshot serves as the baseline for comparing results to those of the Top 20% in the client's industry.

2. Business structure and entities

You can't benchmark properly unless you understand how the business is set up. This means documenting:

- Entity types (company, trust, partnership, sole trader).
- Directors, shareholders, trustees, and beneficiaries.
- Linked entities (and whether they operate commercially or hold assets).

The goal here is to avoid treating the business as a black box. You want a clear map of how it operates and who's involved.

3. Client wants and aspirations

Numbers are only half the story. To make your benchmarking advice relevant, you need to understand what matters most to the client. Use the **Interview Checklist** to uncover their priorities, such as:

- Increasing profit or sales.
- Improving cash flow.
- Protecting assets.
- Reducing workload and stress.
- Achieving personal or lifestyle goals.

This ensures the improvement strategies you recommend are tied directly to outcomes the client values.

Key point: Incorrect information can lead to erroneous conclusions. The correct information gives you clarity, confidence, and credibility.

Your job in Step 2 is simple — get the facts straight. Everything else in the Top 20% Business Benchmarking process depends on it.

Interview checklist

The Interview Checklist is your non-negotiable starting point for benchmarking.

It gives you two things you can't operate without:

1. The client's current financial position – the hard numbers.
2. The client's wants – what matters to them and what they want to achieve.

Miss either of these and you're flying blind. Guesswork doesn't cut it in the Top 20% Business Benchmarking process.

Who do you complete it for?

- All business clients – 100%, no exceptions.
- Individual high-income earners, rental property owners, and the asset-rich, because complexity and opportunity go hand-in-hand.

When you complete it

Do it **face-to-face** when the client is in for their compliance tax meeting. That's the most efficient time — the client's there, the records are open, and you can dig into anything unclear.

If that's not possible, send it by email with clear instructions. Make it easy for them to complete and return before the meeting.

Time commitment:

- First year: 10–15 minutes per client.
- Every year after: Just update it — usually 5 minutes.

This is a habit worth building. Once you've done it once, it's quick, painless, and massively valuable.

Key Point:
- The Interview Checklist isn't admin.
- It's the foundation of the entire benchmarking process — skip it and you're building on sand.

Essential client information

You can't benchmark a business against the Top 20% if you don't have the right information. And by "right," I mean complete, accurate, and relevant. Anything less, and your benchmarks — and your advice — will be wrong.

The aim here is simple — get the facts on the table so you can:
- See exactly where the business is starting from.
- Compare their results to the Top 20% in their industry.
- Pinpoint the most significant gaps and the fastest wins.

The information you need every time:

1. Financial performance (in the exact order used in the TaxFitness software)
- Revenue
- Cost of goods sold (COGS)
- Subcontractors
- Rent
- Wages
- Overheads
- Owner's compensation (separate from wages)
- Net profit before tax

2. Client wants
- The client's priorities and what they want to achieve.
- Short-term and long-term goals.
- Specific improvement targets — profit, sales, cash flow, hours worked, lifestyle, asset protection, succession, or exit plans.

Why it matters

Incorrect data leads to an incorrect benchmark.

Using the wrong benchmark can lead to incorrect conclusions. Drawing incorrect conclusions means the client won't act.

When you've got the correct information, you can:

- Show exactly how the business compares to the top performers in their industry.
- Put a dollar figure on the improvement opportunity.
- Recommend strategies that are both relevant and achievable — and get the client's buy-in.

Key point:

- Accurate information = accurate benchmarks.
- Accurate benchmarks = advice the client will act on.

Reasons why we gather the client information

If you don't have the correct information, you can't run an accurate benchmark, and you can't advise the client to act on it. It's that simple.

Gathering client information isn't an admin exercise. It's the foundation of the Top 20% Business Benchmarking process. Without it, you're guessing — and when you guess, you miss.

We collect this information for four clear reasons:

1. To understand the client's current position

You can't show a client where they can go until you know precisely where they are now. Accurate data provides a baseline — including revenue, costs, profit, and the performance drivers that matter. This is the starting point for every benchmark comparison.

2. To identify gaps against the top 20%

Benchmarking works because it measures performance against

the best in the industry. With the correct information, you can pinpoint exactly where the client is underperforming — and by how much. This turns vague "improvement" into measurable targets in dollars and percentages.

3. To link advice to what the client wants

Data is useless if it's not connected to the client's priorities. By collecting both financial facts and the client's wants, you can make sure your recommendations are relevant — and that the client sees the direct link between action and results they care about.

4. To build trust and credibility

When you know the client's situation in detail, you can talk with authority. It shows you've done the work, you understand their business, and you're not just delivering generic advice. That's how you earn buy-in and long-term engagement.

Key point:
- We don't gather information for the sake of it.
- We gather it because, without it, accurate benchmarking and meaningful advice are impossible.

Methods of gathering information efficiently

Information gathering doesn't have to be slow, painful, or disruptive. If it takes too long, it won't get done, and without accurate information, you can't run a meaningful benchmark.

The key is to systemise and streamline how you collect the data so it's quick for you, easy for the client, and consistent every time.

Here are the most efficient methods:

1. Complete the Interview Checklist in a face-to-face or video meeting

The fastest and most accurate way to gather information is to walk the client through the Interview Checklist in real time — either:

- Face-to-face during their compliance tax meeting or annual review.
- Via video call using Zoom, Teams, or similar, for clients who can't come into the office.

Advantages:

- You control the flow of the conversation.
- You can clarify answers instantly.
- You capture all the details in one sitting.

2. Pre-meeting email of the checklist

If a real-time meeting isn't possible, email the Interview Checklist ahead of time with:

- Clear instructions on how to complete it.
- A deadline for return.
- The option to attach supporting documents at the same time.

This prompts the client to consider their financial position and priorities before your review.

3. Leverage existing data

Much of the information you need is already sitting in your accounting software or client records.

- Pull the last 12 months of financials to pre-fill revenue, COGS, wages, rent, and other benchmark inputs.
- Use last year's benchmarking report to identify missing or updated data points.

Pre-filling reduces client effort and speeds up the process.

4. Direct data import from Xero, MYOB, and QuickBooks
TaxFitness allows you to pull client financial data directly from major accounting platforms, removing the need for manual entry:

- Xero – import actual financials instantly.
- MYOB – load the numbers in a few clicks.
- QuickBooks – bring in accurate, up-to-date client data without rekeying.

Data import is the quickest and most accurate way to get the numbers, especially for annual updates.

5. Use a consistent format
Always use the same version of the Interview Checklist for every client.

- Keeps the process standardised.
- Makes year-on-year comparisons easy.
- Minimises the risk of missing data.

6. Update annually, don't start from scratch
In year one, the checklist takes 10–15 minutes per client. In future years, you update changes — usually in 5 minutes. This keeps the process sustainable and the data fresh without wasting time.

Key point:

- Whether it's face-to-face, on video, via pre-fill, or direct data import, the method doesn't matter — accuracy and consistency do.
- Get the correct information quickly, and you can benchmark with confidence.

Common challenges and how to overcome them

Even with the right tools and processes, information gathering isn't always smooth. Clients can be busy, distracted, or reluctant to share details. Sometimes the data is incomplete, inconsistent, or simply incorrect.

If you don't deal with these issues, you end up with benchmarks built on shaky foundations — and that kills credibility.

Here are the most common challenges and how to deal with them:

1. Clients don't return the checklist
The problem: You send the Interview Checklist, and it vanishes into thin air. No reply. No data. No progress.

The fix:
- Book a face-to-face or video meeting to complete it together.
- If sending it by email, set a clear deadline and follow up within a week.
- Explain why you need it — connect the checklist to better advice, bigger opportunities, and more profit for the client.

2. Incomplete or vague answers
The problem: Clients often provide half-answers or estimates instead of actual numbers.

The fix:
- Pre-fill as much as possible from accounting software or prior reports.
- In meetings, probe with follow-up questions until you get specifics.
- If numbers are missing, assign the client a short action list to send them through before the benchmark is run.

3. Outdated or inaccurate data

The problem: The numbers don't reflect the current year — or worse, they're wrong.

The fix:
- Pull the latest data directly from Xero, MYOB, or Quick-Books to remove human error.
- Cross-check against the most recent BAS, P&L, or management accounts.
- Only benchmark against complete and current data — no shortcuts.

4. Client pushback on sharing information

The problem: Some clients are hesitant to share detailed personal or business data.

The fix:
- Build trust by explaining confidentiality and how the data is used purely for benchmarking.
- Focus on what's in it for them — better comparisons, clear improvement targets, and measurable results.
- Share an example of a benchmarking success story to prove the value.

5. The process takes too long

The problem: Time blowouts kill momentum for you and the client.

The fix:
- Use direct data imports and pre-fills to slash completion time.
- Keep to the checklist — no irrelevant side questions.
- Update annually instead of starting from scratch.

Key point:
- Challenges are only problems if you let them slow you down.
- The solution is always the same — make it easy, make it quick, and make sure the client understands the value.

Ensuring data accuracy and integrity

Inaccurate or incomplete data destroys the credibility of benchmarking advice. If the numbers are wrong, the insights will be wrong — and once a client loses confidence in your figures, it's an uphill battle to win it back. As professionals, we have a responsibility to ensure that every data point is accurate, consistent, and verifiable before it is incorporated into the benchmarking process.

The integrity of your advice starts here. Top 20% benchmarks are only powerful when the inputs are rock-solid. That means no guesswork, no shortcuts, and no blind acceptance of the figures provided.

1. Use reliable data sources
Only work with data drawn from primary, verifiable sources:
- Accounting software exports – Direct from Xero, MYOB, QuickBooks (using TaxFitness direct import where possible to eliminate manual entry errors).
- Official financial statements – Audited or reviewed where available.
- Bank statements – To cross-check revenue and expense totals.
- Source documents – Invoices, payroll reports, and lease agreements.

2. Standardise data entry
Minor inconsistencies can skew results significantly. Establish

clear standards for:

- Chart of accounts mapping to the TaxFitness benchmarking categories.
- Treatment of owner's salary and drawings.
- Allocation of subcontractor costs vs wages.
- Handling one-off or extraordinary items.

3. Validate before you analyse

Always run an initial "sense check":

- Compare year-on-year variances and investigate anomalies.
- Cross-check gross margins, wage percentages, and net profit margins against industry norms before proceeding.
- Confirm that totals (e.g., COGS + wages + rent + overheads + owner's compensation + net profit) add to 100% in your KPI model.

4. Detect and eliminate errors early

Build a culture of accuracy by:

- Using reconciliation reports to identify discrepancies.
- Reviewing unusual trends or spikes in expense categories.
- Confirming that the reporting period matches the benchmark period (12 months, full financial year).

5. Protect data integrity

Clients must trust that their information is handled securely:

- Store all client data in secure, access-controlled systems (in line with legal and professional obligations).
- Keep an audit trail of changes to figures.
- Use version control when working with multiple iterations of data.

6. Avoid "Garbage In, Garbage Out"

The Top 20% Business Benchmarking System is only as good as the data that feeds it. Taking time up front to check and clean data is far more efficient than reworking flawed reports later. Remember, your recommendations will drive significant business decisions — accuracy isn't optional.

Key principle: If you wouldn't rely on the data to make a significant financial decision in your own business, it's not ready for your client's benchmarking report.

Confidentiality and ethical considerations

When clients provide you with their financial information, they are placing an extraordinary level of trust in you. They are effectively opening the books on their livelihood, their investment, and often their family's financial future. That trust is not negotiable — it's the foundation of a professional relationship and must be safeguarded at all times.

Benchmarking advice is not just about numbers. It's about utilising privileged information to assist clients in making informed decisions. The way you handle that information reflects directly on your professionalism, integrity, and the reputation of your practice.

1. Maintain absolute confidentiality

Client data is not to be shared, discussed, or displayed outside authorised channels:

- Never disclose specific figures to third parties without explicit client consent.
- Avoid any identifiable comparisons when using examples in training, presentations, or marketing.
- Use anonymised or aggregated data when demonstrating benchmarking outcomes to prospects.

2. Comply with legal and professional obligations

As accountants and advisors, we are bound by:

- Privacy laws – Compliance with the Privacy Act 1988 (Cth) and the Australian Privacy Principles (or equivalent legislation in other jurisdictions).
- Professional codes of ethics – CA ANZ, CPA Australia, IPA standards.
- Engagement agreements – Adhering to the scope and conditions outlined in your engagement letters.

3. Secure data handling

Confidentiality isn't just about keeping quiet — it's about protecting information physically and digitally:

- Store data in secure, encrypted systems with restricted access.
- Use password-protected devices and multi-factor authentication for all benchmarking tools.
- Avoid transmitting sensitive information via unsecured channels such as unencrypted email.

4. Respect the client relationship

Ethical behaviour extends beyond compliance:

- Be transparent about how their data will be used and who will have access.
- Avoid conflicts of interest — if you are benchmarking for competing businesses, manage and disclose appropriately.
- Use the data solely for the purpose it was collected — delivering value through accurate benchmarking advice.

5. Handle benchmark comparisons responsibly

Top 20% benchmarks are powerful — but they must be used with care:

- Never use benchmarking results to make negative or disparaging comments about a client's business.
- Position insights as constructive and forward-looking, with the goal of improvement.
- Ensure that any comparative data you share with the client is accurate, relevant, and presented in context.

Key principle: Confidentiality and ethics are not "add-ons" to the benchmarking process — they are at the very heart of it. Lose them, and you lose the client's trust, your professional standing, and potentially your licence to practise.

Workflow for Step 2 – Information gathering

A great benchmarking report starts with great data. Step 2 of the TaxFitness Top 20% Business Benchmarking System involves gathering, verifying, and organising the information that forms the foundation of your analysis. The workflow needs to be structured, consistent, and repeatable so every client receives the same high standard of accuracy and insight.

Below is the recommended workflow to follow every time.

1. Prepare for data collection

- Confirm the engagement – Ensure you have a signed engagement letter covering benchmarking services and data use.
- Send client checklist – So the client knows precisely what to prepare.
- Schedule the meeting – Set a date for a face-to-face or video interview (aim to complete within one week of sending the checklist).

2. Gather client information

Method options:

- Direct interview – Ask questions, clarify anomalies, and record answers in real time.
- Software integration – Use TaxFitness direct data imports from Xero, MYOB, or QuickBooks to pull figures without manual entry.
- Document upload – Have clients securely upload financial statements, bank statements, payroll reports, and key contracts.

3. Validate and cross-check data

Reconcile totals from accounting software with bank statements or source documents.

- Confirm that the chart of accounts mapping matches the TaxFitness benchmarking categories.
- Investigate any unusual or inconsistent figures before moving forward.

4. Identify client priorities

During the interview, capture:

- The client's key business goals.
- Problem areas they want to address.
- Opportunities they're curious about.

This ensures your benchmarking advice is aligned with what's important to them, not just what the numbers say.

5. Record data in TaxFitness

- Enter validated figures into the TaxFitness benchmarking tool (or import directly).
- Ensure all KPI categories add up correctly — COGS, wages,

rent, subcontractors, overheads, owner's compensation, and net profit should total 100%.

- Tag the client record with relevant notes, goals, and exceptional circumstances.

6. Quality control review
- Double-check all inputs for accuracy.
- Confirm the reporting period matches the Top 20% benchmark dataset.
- Have a second team member review the data where possible.

7. Secure and store data
- Save client records in a secure, access-controlled environment.
- Keep an audit trail of changes for transparency and compliance.

Key principle: The goal of Step 2 is not just to collect data — it's to collect the correct data, in the proper format, at the highest level of accuracy so the insights you deliver are trusted, actionable, and aligned with the client's priorities.

7

Step 3 - Fees and charging clients

'DO WHAT YOU CAN, WITH WHAT YOU HAVE, WHERE YOU ARE'
– THEODORE ROOSEVELT (26TH PRESIDENT OF THE UNITED
STATES, SOLDIER, CONSERVATIONIST, AND PROGRESSIVE
REFORMER, EARLY 1900S).

You are at STEP 3

Step 1: Systems and practice	Step 2: Information gathering	**Step 3: Fees and charging clients**
Step 4: Educate clients	Step 5: Sell service to clients	Step 6: The two TaxFitness databases
Step 7: Select business advisory strategies	Step 8: Top 20% Business Benchmarking Report	Step 9: Advisory meeting (report presentation)
Step 10: Implementing strategies		

The objective of fees and charging clients

In the Top 20% Business Benchmarking System, fees are not just about "covering costs" or "billing for time." They are a deliberate, strategic tool that positions you as a high-value adviser, ensures your services are sustainable, and signals to clients the quality and outcomes they can expect.

The objective is threefold:

1. Generate significant, predictable revenue

For an advisory service to thrive, it must produce meaningful income from day one. In the Top 20% model, that means an additional **$30,000 to $100,000 in fees in the first year**—not in five years, not "eventually," but now. This is achievable because you're delivering premium insights that directly improve your clients' profits and competitiveness. The fee structure must reflect that value from the outset.

2. Reinforce the value of your service
The way you price sends a message. Undercharging signals "low value" and attracts price-sensitive clients who are less likely to implement your advice. Charging appropriately—based on outcomes, not hours—reinforces that this is a results-driven, high-impact service. Clients pay for improvement, not just analysis, and the fee confirms they're investing, not a purchase.

3. Build a scalable, professional advisory division
Advisory should be a profit centre in its own right, not a free add-on to compliance. The objective of fees and charging is to create a model that can be repeated with every suitable client, handled by your team, and scaled without eroding margins. That means clear pricing systems, consistent proposals, and a structure that avoids "negotiating down" your worth.

In short, your pricing is the spine of your advisory business. Get it wrong, and you're stuck in "helping for free" mode. Get it right, and you have a professional, respected, and profitable Top 20% service that clients value, staff can deliver, and your firm can grow year after year.

Business benchmarking price list
The Top 20% Business Benchmarking service is a premium, insight-driven advisory product designed to position your firm as a trusted growth partner — not just a compliance provider.

The following price guide offers a clear and scalable framework for determining fees based on client size and the scope of service. All fees are **exclusive of GST.**

1. Profit Transformation Program (Monthly benchmarking & advisory implementation – minimum 12-month contract).

Purpose: High-touch transformational program combining benchmarking, advisory, and accountability.

Inclusions:
- Monthly KPI benchmarking and trend analysis.
- Monthly improvement sessions (in person or online).
- Full implementation support for improvement strategies.
- Accountability and progress tracking.
- Unlimited phone and email support between meetings.

Fee structure (per month):
- Small business (up to $200,000 turnover): $600
- Medium business ($200,001 – $500,000 turnover): $1,000
- Large business ($500,001 – $1,500,000 turnover): $1,600
- Large business ($1,500,001 – $3,000,000 turnover): $2,400
- Large business ($3,000,001+ turnover): $4,000

2. Performance Growth Programme (Quarterly benchmarking – minimum 12 months).

Purpose: Ongoing performance improvement with regular tracking and accountability.

Inclusions:
- Updated benchmarking every quarter.
- Quarterly business benchmarking report and variance analysis.
- 60 – 90 minute quarterly strategy meetings.
- Tracking of progress towards Top 20% performance.
- Accountability for agreed actions between meetings.

Fee structure (per quarter):
- Small business (up to $200,000 turnover): $1,000 – $1,500
- Medium business ($200,001 – $500,000 turnover): $2,000
- Large business ($500,001 – $1,500,000 turnover): $2,500
- Large business ($1,500,001 – $3,000,000 turnover): $3,000
- Large business ($3,000,001+ turnover): $5,000

3. Top 20% Strategic Performance Review (Annual benchmarking review & 12-month plan)

Purpose: Annual review of performance and strategic reset.

Inclusions:
- 12-month KPI review against Top 20% benchmarks.
- Updated business benchmarking report.
- Strategic workshop to review progress and set goals.
- 12-month action plan for growth and improvement.

Fee structure:
- Small business (up to $200,000 turnover): $1,000 – $1,500
- Medium business ($200,001 – $500,000 turnover): $2,000
- Large business ($500,001 – $1,500,000 turnover): $2,500
- Large business ($1,500,001 – $3,000,000 turnover): $3,000
- Large business ($3,000,001+ turnover): $5,000

4. Top 20% Performance Diagnostic (Initial benchmarking assessment – one off).

Purpose: First-time, complete diagnostic benchmarking analysis.

Inclusions:
- First-time benchmarking of the business against the Top 20% KPI's.
- Full data gathering and KPI analysis.
- Comprehensive business benchmarking report.
- 60–90 minute results meeting and action plan.
- Action plan to address performance groups.

Fee structure:
- Small business (up to $200,000 turnover): $1,000 – $1,500
- Medium business ($200,001 – $500,000 turnover): $2,000
- Large business ($500,001 – $1,500,000 turnover): $2,500
- Large business ($1,500,001 – $3,000,000 turnover): $3,000
- Large business ($3,000,001+ turnover): $5,000

5. Top 20% Industry Insights Report

Purpose: Spark client interest and demonstrate your expertise.

Inclusions:
- Professionally presented fact sheet of Top 20% industry KPI's.
- Definitions of key performance measures.
- 3–5 quick win improvement ideas.

When to use:
- Can be used with current clients or prospects to start the advisory conversation.

Fee: Complimentary.

Implementation tip: Always present the highest-value program first when discussing pricing. This anchors the client's perception of value, making all other packages appear more affordable. Use the Top 20% industry fact sheet as a no-obligation conversation starter, then progress clients into paid benchmarking packages.

Pricing systems & basis

The way you set your pricing for **Top 20% Business Benchmarking** services sends an unequivocal message to clients about the value of your advice. Get it right, and clients will see you as a strategic partner who drives measurable profit improvements. Get it wrong, and you risk being viewed as just another cost.

Pricing must be based on three key factors:
1. Value delivered, not hours spent.
2. Clarity in scope and outcomes.
3. Alignment with the client's perception of ROI.

1. Value-based pricing – the benchmarking standard

Value-based pricing is the most effective model for Top 20% benchmarking because it ties your fee to the financial upside you help deliver — not to the number of hours you spend crunching numbers.

Example:

If benchmarking reveals that improving COGS and wage ratios to Top 20% levels will increase a client's profit by $120,000 a year, charging $6,000 – $12,000 for the program is highly justifiable. Clients will happily invest $1 to make $10.

Advantages:
- Rewards expertise, not effort.
- Positions benchmarking as an investment, not an expense.
- Enables premium fees for high-impact advice.

2. Tiered pricing – options, not discounts

Offer 2–4 distinct service levels (e.g., transformation program, quarterly program, one-off analysis, fact sheet only). This creates a "Good/ Better / Best" choice structure that allows clients to self-select based on ambition and budget.

Pro tip: Always lead with your most comprehensive package — it sets the value anchor for all other options.

3. Fixed-fee packages – confidence for both sides

Benchmarking works best when clients know the exact cost upfront. Fixed fees:
- Eliminate fee disputes.
- Make it easier to sell ongoing programs.
- Allow clients to commit without fear of "surprise" invoices.

Your fixed fee should cover:
- Data gathering and analysis.
- Report preparation.
- Client presentation meetings.
- Follow-up and accountability check-ins (if included in package).

4. Bundled advisory pricing – increase the lifetime value

Consider bundling benchmarking with complementary services, such as tax planning, cash flow forecasting, or strategic planning sessions.

This:
- Makes the package more valuable.
- Locks in the client for multiple services.
- Increases annual revenue per client without adding significant delivery time.

5. Review and adjust annually
Your pricing should not be static. As your expertise, processes, and client results improve, your fees should increase accordingly.

A good rule of thumb:
- Review your benchmarking pricing every 12 months.
- Increase fees in line with the additional value you deliver and the market positioning you want to maintain.

Implementation tip
Never start the pricing conversation with "what would you like to pay?" or "how much can you afford?". Instead, lead with:
- The performance gap you've identified.
- The profit improvement potential.
- The roadmap for closing that gap.
- Then present your fee as a fraction of the upside.

Why value-based pricing works best for Top 20% benchmarking

Top 20% Business Benchmarking is not about selling reports — it's about delivering profit transformation. When you show a business owner exactly how far they are from the industry's best performers, and then provide a clear roadmap to close that gap, you're not selling "time" — you're selling results.

1. The client sees a return, not a cost
In benchmarking, it's common to uncover six-figure improvement opportunities — often without significant structural change. If a client can see that implementing your recommendations could add $80,000, $150,000, or even $250,000 to their bottom line, paying you $5,000 to $15,000 feels like a smart business move. It shifts the mindset from **"How much does it cost?" to "How quickly can we get started?"**

2. It rewards expertise, not effort
An average accountant might spend 10 hours preparing a benchmarking analysis. A seasoned advisor using the TaxFitness system can deliver a far more insightful report in half the time — but with double the impact. If you bill by the hour, working faster can cost you more. If you price by value, efficiency becomes your profit advantage.

3. It aligns incentives
Value-based pricing makes you and the client partners in success. The more improvement you help them achieve, the more they see your fee as an investment rather than an overhead. It fosters a long-term relationship — clients stay because they can track progress quarter after quarter.

4. It positions benchmarking as a premium advisory
Hourly billing or low fixed fees signal to clients that benchmarking is just another "add-on" report. Value-based pricing positions it as a **core strategic service** — the type of service top-performing businesses actively seek out. This supports higher fees, more substantial margins, and better client retention.

5. It encourages commitment and action

When clients make a meaningful investment in the service, they are more likely to act on the recommendations. A low-fee, low-commitment benchmarking report often ends up in a drawer. Value-based pricing ensures the client has a stake in the outcome — and that drives real results.

Bottom line: Benchmarking done well is worth far more than the hours spent preparing it. With value-based pricing, you're paid for your expertise, your insights, and the financial transformation you deliver — not just your time.

Fee fundamentals

Benchmarking is not a low-value add-on to compliance. It's a premium, results-focused advisory service that helps clients generate more revenue, increase efficiency, and outperform their competitors. Your fees should reflect that.

When it comes to Top 20% Business Benchmarking, there are several non-negotiable fundamentals every accountant must understand and apply:

1. Price for value, not time

- If you charge by the hour, you're selling effort. If you charge for value, you're selling outcomes. A benchmarking engagement might take you five hours to complete — but if it uncovers a $150,000 annual profit improvement, the client is paying for that $150,000 outcome, not the five hours.

2. Anchor high, then offer options

- Always present your premium service first. This sets the anchor in the client's mind, making lower-priced options appear more affordable. Present the Profit Transformation

Program first, followed by quarterly, annual, and one-off options.

3. Be clear and upfront
- Clients should know exactly:
- What's included in the service.
- What results can they expect?
- How much will it cost?
- Clarity removes fee resistance and builds trust. Avoid vague scopes or "hourly rates" that lead to uncertainty.

4. Separate advisory from compliance
- Never bundle benchmarking into compliance for free or at a token fee. If you include it without charging, you devalue the service and train clients to expect high-value insights for nothing. Benchmarking should be included in your advisory service menu — priced and positioned as a standalone product.

5. Match fees to client size and complexity
- A $3 million turnover business has more moving parts, more data to analyse, and greater upside potential than a $200,000 turnover business — and your pricing should reflect that. Tiered pricing by turnover ensures fairness, profitability, and scalability.

6. Link fees to ROI in the client's mind
- When you can show that your fee is a fraction of the financial improvement possible, resistance drops. If your fee is $5,000 and the improvement potential is $ 100,000 or more, the conversation shifts from "That's expensive" to "That's a smart investment."

7. Review and increase regularly

Your benchmarking expertise, systems, and client results will improve over time — your pricing should too. Review your fees annually and increase them in line with:

- The value you deliver.
- Your positioning in the market.
- The demand for your service.

Bottom line:

Benchmarking fees are a direct reflection of the value you place on your expertise. If you undervalue your service, clients will too. Price confidently, deliver exceptional results, and your benchmarking division will quickly become one of the most profitable areas of your practice.

Psychology of pricing

Pricing is never just about the number on the page. How you **present** your fee can be as important as the amount itself. The correct pricing psychology positions your benchmarking service as premium, high-value, and worth every dollar — without triggering unnecessary price resistance.

1. Anchor high

Humans tend to compare prices relative to the first figure they encounter. By presenting your **highest-value package first** (e.g., Profit Transformation Program), you set the "anchor" in the client's mind. When you then show the quarterly or annual options, they appear more affordable by comparison.

2. Offer three or four options

People like choice, but too much choice leads to indecision. The sweet spot is **three or four clearly defined packages:**

- Premium (best results, highest investment)
- Mid-tier (good results, medium investment)
- Entry-level (lower results, lowest investment)

Most clients naturally choose the middle option, which is often the most profitable for you.

3. Price in ranges where appropriate
For some services (such as small business benchmarking), provide a range (e.g., $1,000–$1,500) rather than a fixed figure. This creates flexibility, allows you to tailor the final fee based on complexity, and removes the perception that you're "locked in" before seeing the data.

4. Frame your fee against the ROI
Never present your price in isolation. Always link it to the potential for improvement. Example: "Your wage costs are 6% above the Top 20% benchmark. If we bring that down, you could save $85,000 a year. The program is $8,000 — so you're effectively investing $1 to make $10."

5. Use the "decoy effect"
Introduce a high-priced package you don't expect many to take. Its primary role is to make your target package look like the best value. Example: If your quarterly program is $8,000/year and your monthly program is $36,000/year, the quarterly option suddenly feels like a bargain.

6. Avoid discounting — add value instead
Discounting erodes perceived value and conditions clients to wait for deals. Instead of lowering your price, add extras:
- An additional KPI analysis.

- A free fact sheet for another business they own.
- An extra follow-up meeting.

7. Make the fee the last thing you say
Lead with:
- The gap between their current performance and the Top 20%.
- The dollar value of fixing that gap.
- The plan to get there.

Only then present your fee, framed as a fraction of the upside.

Bottom line: The psychology of pricing is about more than numbers — it's about positioning, perception, and persuasion. Present your fees strategically, and you'll find clients are far more willing to commit to premium benchmarking services.

Benchmarking fee presentation script

Purpose: Give accountants a clear, repeatable structure for presenting Top 20% Business Benchmarking fees in a way that positions the service as an investment — not a cost — and maximises client acceptance rates.

Step 1 – **Frame the performance gap.**
"Based on your numbers, your gross profit margin is 7% lower than the Top 20% in your industry. That's about $140,000 in potential extra profit each year that you're currently not capturing."

Why: This makes the gap tangible and dollar-based before mentioning price. Clients are now focused on the upside, not the cost.

Step 2 – Outline the improvement plan.
"We can close that gap by focusing on a few key areas — reducing the cost of goods, improving labour efficiency, and adjusting pricing. Our benchmarking program is designed to identify the exact actions needed and track your progress over time."

Why: This positions you as the problem-solver with a proven system — not someone selling a "report."

Step 3 – Anchor with the premium option first
"We have a few different service levels. The most comprehensive program is our **Profit Transformation Program**, priced at $4,000 per month for large businesses. It includes monthly KPI benchmarking, monthly improvement sessions, unlimited support, and full accountability to make sure changes get implemented."

Why: This sets the high anchor so other options feel more affordable.

Step 4 – Present the mid-tier option as the best value
"The option most of our clients choose is our **Performance Growth Program**. It's $3,000 per quarter for your size of business — that's $12,000 a year. You still get quarterly reporting, strategy meetings, and action plans, but at a lower frequency."

Why: This uses the "middle choice" effect and positions your most profitable tier as the logical choice.

Step 5 – Offer the entry-level option
"If you'd prefer to start smaller, we can do a **Top 20% Performance Diagnostic** for $3,000. That's a full diagnostic with an action plan — but you'd need to track and implement changes yourself after that."

Why: This ensures there's always an accessible entry point, but without undermining the value of ongoing programs.

Step 6 – Reframe fee as ROI
"The quarterly program is $12,000 a year. If we can close even half of that $140,000 profit gap, you're looking at a 5–6 times return on investment in the first year alone."

Why: ROI framing makes the fee look small compared to the gain.

Step 7 – Pause and let them respond
After delivering the ROI statement, stay silent. Give the client space to process and respond.

Pro tip: The first person to speak usually concedes — so let them be the one.

Step 8 – Address concerns with confidence
If they hesitate on price:

"That's exactly why you need this program. You can't afford to leave $140,000 on the table each year. We'll make sure you get the results to justify the investment many times over."

Final note: Never apologise for your fees. You're not selling hours; you're selling a proven pathway to higher profits, more substantial cash flow, and a more valuable business. The price should always feel like a fraction of the upside.

Structuring and presenting prices

If you want clients to invest in your **Top 20% Business Bench-marking** services, you can't just "mention a price" and hope they say yes. The way you **package, name, and present** your pricing determines whether a client sees it as a wise business decision or just another bill.

1. Lead with the most transformational option

Open with your **highest-value package** — the one that delivers the most significant improvement in profits, cash flow, and business performance. Why? Because it sets the value anchor. Every other option will feel like great value in comparison.

2. Present clear, comparable packages

Use a **Good / Better / Best** format so clients can quickly compare scope, frequency, and investment.

- Best: Full transformation (monthly program).
- Better: Consistent improvement (quarterly program)
- Good: Strategic performance review (annually)
- Good: One-off analysis to get started

This structure simplifies the decision and eliminates uncertainty.

3. Name packages for the outcome, not the Process

Forget bland names like "Option 1" or "Quarterly Service." Your packages should make the client want the result.

Examples:
- Profit Transformation Program (monthly).
- Performance Growth Program (quarterly).
- Top 20% Strategic Performance Review (annually).
- Top 20% Performance Diagnostic (one-off)

Outcome-driven names make your service sound like a solution, not a product.

4. Highlight only the inclusions that matter
Don't drown clients in 15 bullet points of detail. List **3–5 high-impact deliverables** per package — the ones that will sway the decision. Keep it lean so they focus on the value, not the "tasks."

5. Make the prices easy to compare visually
Use a simple table or grid showing:
- Package name
- Key inclusions (3–5 bullets)
- Price (ex GST)
- Payment terms (per month, quarter, year)

When clients can see the progression from Good → Better → Best, they're more likely to step up to the higher-value option.

6. Close by tying the price back to the profit gap
Once you've presented the packages, bring them back to the numbers:

"The quarterly program is $12,000 a year. Even if we close only half of your $140,000 profit gap, you're looking at a 5-6 times return on your investment."

When you frame it this way, the decision becomes less about cost and more about missed opportunity.

Bottom line: Your pricing isn't just a number — it's a positioning tool. Package it strategically, present it with authority, and always tie it back to the potential for profit improvement. That's how you move clients from "thinking about it" to **signing today**.

Overcoming pricing objections

Pricing objections are not a sign your service is overpriced — they are a sign your client hasn't yet connected the value to the investment. In Top 20% Business Benchmarking, our role is to shift the conversation from "What does it cost?" to "What will it return?"

1. Anchor in results, not cost

When a client hesitates, they are often thinking in terms of cost rather than return on investment.

"This isn't an expense. It's an investment with measurable outcomes." Reinforce real-world results: "Our benchmarking process regularly identifies $50k–$200k in extra profit for clients in your industry. If we deliver even half of that, the service pays for itself many times over."

2. Use comparisons they understand

Clients need context. Relate your fee to something they already spend money on — and that has less tangible return.

"You invest more in rent or insurance each month, and neither of those directly increases your profit. This does."

3. Break down the numbers

Large numbers create resistance. Smaller, bite-sized numbers create clarity. For example, if the annual benchmarking review and strategic plan is $6,000/year:

- That's $500/month
- Or $115/week — the equivalent of one dinner for two. Now, match it with an expected ROI figure.

4. De-risk the decision

Offer a clear path where the perceived risk is lower than the perceived benefit.

Examples:

- First-year profit guarantee: "If we don't identify improvements worth at least our fee, you don't pay the full amount."
- Staged commitment: Start with the initial benchmarking assessment before the complete annual program.

5. Reframe "too expensive"

If you hear "It's too expensive," what they're saying is "I'm not convinced it's worth it." Your job is to:

- Restate the problem they face (low margins, poor cash flow, stagnant growth).
- Quantify the impact of leaving it unresolved. Demonstrate how your benchmarking process addresses it more efficiently, cost-effectively, and with measurable certainty compared to relying on guesswork.

6. Bring evidence

Nothing dissolves scepticism like proof. Bring:

- Industry Top 20% benchmark data for their sector
- Case studies showing profit increases from similar businesses
- Specific advisory insights they will gain in the first session

7. Control the timing of price discussions

Price should not be the first thing they hear. Follow this sequence:

- Discover the problem and its cost to them.
- Show the gap between their current position and the Top 20%.
- Outline your process and results.
- Present the price after the value is clear.

Tip: When a client pushes back on price, don't argue. Slow down, ask questions, and reconnect them with why they were interested in the first place. Objections are invitations for better explanations, not battles to be won.

Building confidence in your pricing

If you're not confident in your price, your client won't be either. Confidence isn't arrogance — it's the quiet certainty that what you're offering delivers far more value than it costs. In Top 20% Business Benchmarking, confidence in your pricing stems from understanding three key factors: value, proof, and delivery.

1. Know the value you create

You can't sell with conviction if you don't believe the numbers yourself. Take the time to:

- Quantify the typical financial uplift your benchmarking uncovers (profit increases, cost savings, productivity gains).
- Understand the strategic value (better decision-making, improved cash flow, reduced risk).
- Translate your service into their language — dollars saved, hours freed, percentage improvements.

When you believe the value outweighs the price many times over, the conversation shifts from "Can they afford it?" to "Can they afford not to?"

2. Master your price story

Don't just state a fee — tell the story behind it. For example:

"Our annual benchmarking and strategic planning package is $6,000. That's based on delivering four deep-dive reviews a year, over 40 KPIs, and specific advisory actions proven to move businesses into the Top 20% in their industry."

When clients see the structure and purpose behind the price, it feels deliberate, not arbitrary.

3. Practice saying your price out loud

If you hesitate, mumble, or immediately discount, you're signalling doubt.

- State your price clearly, without apology or explanation.
- Pause and let it land.
- Answer questions, but don't rush to fill the silence — confidence grows in the pause.

4. Back it with proof

Confidence comes from having evidence ready:

- Case studies showing measurable ROI
- Testimonials from clients in similar industries
- Before-and-after benchmarks demonstrating transformation

When you can point to real-world wins, your price becomes a reflection of proven results, not a gamble.

5. Avoid price apologies

Phrases like "I know it's a lot" or "We can make it cheaper" erode trust. Instead, reinforce value:

"This investment is designed to generate at least three to five times the return in your first year."

6. Benchmark your price

Remember — in the advisory space, premium services command premium pricing. Position yourself alongside other high-value providers, not bargain operators. If your price is significantly lower than comparable high-performance offerings, the client will question your capability rather than celebrate the discount.

Tip: You can't build confidence in your price overnight. It comes from preparation, proof, and practice. The more you believe in your service, the more your clients will believe it's worth every cent.

Implementation and review

Setting your prices is not a one-time decision — it's a process of implementation, monitoring, and adjustment. In Top 20% Business Benchmarking, the way you introduce your pricing to the market and review it over time can have just as much impact on profitability as the price itself.

1. Roll out pricing with intention

When you've set a new or updated fee structure:
- Inform your team: Everyone needs to know the pricing, inclusions, and value story so it's presented consistently.
- Update all collateral: Price lists, proposal templates, website copy, and any bundled service packages must match the new structure.
- Communicate to existing clients: For current clients, explain the change in terms of increased value, improved service, and enhanced results.

2. Test and refine in the market

Rather than waiting years to adjust, monitor client reactions from day one:
- Which packages are most frequently chosen?
- Where do prospects hesitate?
- Are you meeting your close rate targets?

Minor tweaks early can prevent bigger revenue losses later.

3. Track pricing KPIs
Measure the success of your pricing, not just your sales:
- Average revenue per client
- Conversion rate (proposals accepted vs proposals sent)
- Gross margin on benchmarking services
- Average discount given (and why)
- Client retention rate post-price change

4. Schedule formal reviews
Your market, competitors, and value offering will evolve — your prices should too.
- Quarterly pulse checks: Review uptake and objections; adjust scripts or value presentation.
- Annual review: Compare your fees to inflation, market positioning, and the value you now deliver.
- Benchmark your pricing: Look at what other premium providers are charging in your niche.

5. Stay ahead of price resistance
By regularly reviewing and refining your pricing approach, you avoid the shock factor of significant, infrequent increases. Smaller, incremental changes are easier for both you and your clients to manage — and they maintain your price confidence in the market.

Tip: Your pricing is a living part of your business model. Implement it decisively, monitor it closely, and adjust it before the market forces you to.

8

Step 4 – Educate clients

'GIVE A MAN A FISH AND YOU FEED HIM FOR A DAY, TEACH A
MAN TO FISH AND YOU FEED HIM FOR A LIFETIME'
– MAIMONIDES (SPANISH PHILOSOPHER, 1135-1204).

You are at STEP 4

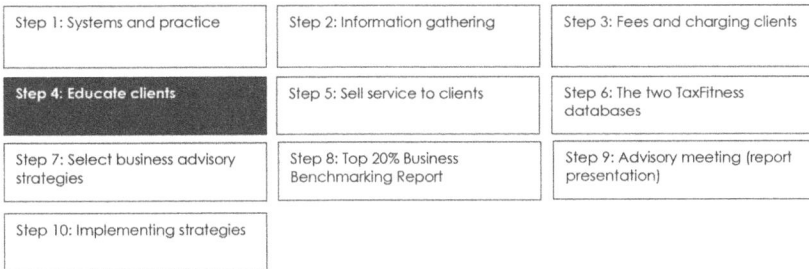

Step 1: Systems and practice	Step 2: Information gathering	Step 3: Fees and charging clients
Step 4: Educate clients	Step 5: Sell service to clients	Step 6: The two TaxFitness databases
Step 7: Select business advisory strategies	Step 8: Top 20% Business Benchmarking Report	Step 9: Advisory meeting (report presentation)
Step 10: Implementing strategies		

The objective of client education

When it comes to business benchmarking, numbers alone don't change a client's behaviour. Education is what turns data into understanding, and understanding into action.

The objective of client education is straightforward: to help clients understand the importance of benchmarking for achieving business success.

Most business owners are time-poor and often overwhelmed by financial information. Without clear guidance, they either ignore the numbers or make decisions based on instinct. By educating clients about the Top 20% benchmarks, you give them a frame of reference:

- What "good" looks like in their industry.
- Where their business currently stands.
- What specific steps can they take to close the gap?

Education transforms benchmarking from being "just another report" into a tool that drives growth, efficiency, and profitability.

Key objectives of client education:

1. Build trust and authority – Education positions you as more than a compliance accountant; you become the business adviser who brings clarity and direction.
2. Drive engagement – An educated client is far more likely to participate in ongoing benchmarking reviews and implement your recommendations.
3. Create demand for advisory services – When clients understand the value of benchmarking, they see the logic in investing in additional services.
4. Improve client outcomes – Education ensures clients act on insights, leading to better business performance – and a stronger advisory relationship.

Why it matters

Uneducated clients rarely act. Educated clients not only understand what's possible, they become motivated to achieve it. That's the difference between a client who "hears" the numbers and one who invests in change.

Your goal is not to impress clients with complex analysis – it's to **make benchmarking accessible, relevant, and repeatable.** When done well, client education becomes the bridge that connects financial data to practical business outcomes.

Explaining the Top 20% benchmarking simply

One of the biggest mistakes accountants make is overcomplicating benchmarking. Clients don't want a lecture on financial ratios or academic models – they want to know, in plain language, "How do we compare, and what should we do about it?"

The objective is to make benchmarking simple, relatable, and client-friendly.

How to frame it

When introducing Top 20% benchmarking, explain it in three steps:

1. Show the benchmark – "Here's what the top 20% of businesses in your industry achieve."
2. Show the gap – "Here's where your business currently sits."
3. Show the opportunity – "If we close that gap, here's what it means in extra profit for you."

That's it. No jargon. No spreadsheets with 40 columns. Just context, clarity, and the potential upside.

What clients need to hear:

- It's not about averages. Average businesses are often struggling. We benchmark against the top 20% because that's where the real profit is.
- It's specific to their industry. These are not generic numbers – they are drawn from actual high-performing businesses in the same field.
- It highlights opportunity, not failure. The purpose isn't to criticise, but to show clients how much better things could be.

The takeaway message

When you explain benchmarking, clients see it as a roadmap, not a report. They don't get lost in numbers – they get motivated by outcomes.

Your job is to make the data real. Put it in their language. Link it to their goals. If a client understands that improving gross profit margin by just 5% could put an extra $150,000 in their pocket, you've done your job.

That's what explaining Top 20% benchmarking is all about: **turning abstract numbers into concrete opportunities.**

Principles of effective education

When it comes to client education, most accountants fall into one of two traps:

- They overwhelm clients with technical jargon.
- They dumb things down so much that the message loses impact.

The sweet spot is clear, simple, and results-driven communication. Clients don't need to know everything you know – they need to understand enough to make better decisions.

Here are the principles that work:

1. Keep it simple

Strip away the noise. Focus only on the three things that matter:

- What the top 20% achieve.
- Where your client sits now.
- What is the gap worth in extra profit?

That's all a business owner wants to know.

2. Make it relevant

Don't talk theory. Don't talk averages. Talk about their industry, their numbers, and their opportunities. The moment a client sees themselves in the picture, the message sticks.

3. Focus on outcomes, not data

Data is interesting. Outcomes are compelling. A client doesn't care that their wages are 6% above benchmark – they care that fixing it could add $80,000 to their bottom line. Always link the numbers to a real outcome.

4. Use stories and comparisons

Stories cut through spreadsheets. Share a case study. Show how another client improved margins. Use a simple "what if" example: "If you operated at top 20% levels, your profit would increase by $150,000." Stories make change believable.

5. Repeat and reinforce

Clients don't get it the first time. Or the second. Education is not a one-off event – it's an ongoing process. Every report, meeting, newsletter, or email should reinforce the same key messages until they are fully understood.

The bottom line

Effective education isn't about teaching clients to be accountants; it's about empowering them to be successful. It's about giving them clarity and motivation to act. Stick to these principles and you'll turn benchmarking from a report they glance at, into a roadmap they follow.

Educational tools & resources

If you want clients to engage with benchmarking, you need the right tools. A good message delivered poorly is ignored. The right tools make your message simple, repeatable, and professional.

Think of these tools as your client education kit. They're not optional extras – they're the levers that turn benchmarking from "numbers in a report" into an ongoing conversation about improvement.

1. Fact sheets & brochures

Every client should receive a simple, one-page fact sheet that explains what Top 20% benchmarking is and why it matters. This isn't marketing fluff – it's education that builds awareness and positions you as the adviser who has the answers.

2. Benchmarking reports & dashboards

The TaxFitness benchmarking report is your most powerful tool. It compares a client's business to the top 20% and highlights the gaps, quantifying the opportunities. Dashboards and charts turn dry data into something visual and easy to grasp.

3. Case studies & success stories

Nothing is more convincing than real examples. Share stories of businesses that lifted performance after benchmarking. Clients tend to connect with other business owners more than with theoretical concepts. "They did it – so can you" is a powerful motivator.

4. Presentations & workshops

A structured presentation – whether one-on-one in a meeting or a group workshop – reinforces your authority and shows professionalism. Slide decks, visual aids, and guided discussions keep the focus on solutions, not spreadsheets.

5. Videos & online content

Short videos or explainer animations are perfect for repetition. Clients can watch them on their own time, and you stay top-of-mind without lifting a finger. An online resource library also adds credibility and scalability to your firm.

6. Regular client communications

Newsletters, email updates, and quarterly reminders keep benchmarking alive between meetings. Each touchpoint reinforces your key messages and educates clients in bite-sized pieces, ensuring a consistent and practical approach to communication.

The bottom line

Clients learn through repetition and variety. A single report won't educate them – but a combination of fact sheets, reports, stories, and consistent communication will. Build your toolkit once, automate as much as possible, and use it with every client.

That's how you scale education, build demand, and position your practice as the authority in business performance.

The power of repetition

We live in a noisy world. In the 1970s, the average person was exposed to about 500 ads a day. Today, it's closer to 10,000. That's marketing clutter on steroids.

Accounting firms aren't immune to this. There are over 800 different products and services marketed to accountants – all promising to boost revenue, cut costs, improve productivity, or grow their client base. Your clients face the same reality: an endless stream of messages competing for their attention.

This is why repetition matters.

One conversation is never enough. Clients don't hear your message the first time – or the second. They only start acting once they've listened to it again and again.

The evidence for repetition

- Microsoft research found the optimal exposure for audio messages was between 6 and 20 times.
- The Rule of Seven says a prospect must hear your message at least seven times before they take action.
- As far back as 1885, Thomas Smith wrote that people ignore the first few exposures, get irritated around the middle, and only start to believe and buy after the 12th to 20th exposure.

The pattern is clear: **frequency builds familiarity, and familiarity builds trust.**

Why clients need repetition

- Noise – They're bombarded with too many competing messages, many of them nonsense.
- Timing – They may not be ready to act right now.
- Price concerns – They're unsure if the return justifies the investment.
- Trust gap – They don't yet believe you can deliver on your promise.

Repetition solves these barriers. The more clients hear your message – consistently, across different formats – the more it cuts through the noise, builds credibility, and positions you as the trusted adviser.

Practical proof

McDonald's has advertised on Australian TV every day for thirty years. Not once. Not occasionally. **Every day.** The result? Instant recognition, ingrained trust, and market dominance.

That's the same principle accountants must apply to benchmarking education. Clients need to see and hear your message – in fact sheets, reports, emails, meetings, videos, and newsletters – not once, but many times.

The Takeaway

Repetition isn't optional – it's essential. If you want clients to understand benchmarking and take action, you need to deliver the message **repeatedly until it resonates with them.**

In advisory services, **the accountant who educates consistently is the one who wins the client's trust, their buy-in, and their business.**

Eight repetition-based marketing strategies

Business owners don't sign up for benchmarking after hearing about it once. They're busy, distracted, and bombarded with other messages. The only way to cut through is repetition – delivering the benchmarking message consistently, in different ways, until it becomes impossible to ignore.

Here's how to make repetition work for Top 20% business benchmarking:

1. Monthly benchmarking emails

Send one benchmarking-focused email each month. Share a Top 20% insight, client success story, or industry comparison.

Example subject lines:
- "How a café lifted profit margins 12% with benchmarking."
- "Are your wages higher than the top 20% in your industry?"

2. Social media drip campaigns (twice a week)

Post regularly on LinkedIn, Facebook, and Instagram to position your firm as the authority on benchmarking. Rotate between:

- Short benchmarking insights (e.g., "Top 20% profit margin in childcare = 18%")
- Client success stories
- Visuals and charts showing gaps and opportunities
- Quick video explainers: "Why the top 20% make twice the profit"

3. Quarterly benchmarking webinars

Run quarterly webinars with themes like:

- "How Top 20% Businesses Double Profits."
- "The 5 Key KPIs That Separate Average from Elite."

End each session with a call-to-action: "Book your benchmarking review to see how your numbers compare."

4. Monthly client newsletter

Send every client a newsletter that keeps benchmarking front of mind. Include:

- Benchmark of the month (one KPI explained in plain language).
- A short case study showing how a client improved results through benchmarking.
- A link to upcoming webinars or resources.

5. Office visuals

Transform your office into a dynamic showcase for benchmarking and performance improvement. Use posters, flyers, and table cards with messages like:

- "The Top 20% of businesses in your industry earn 2x the profit. Where do you sit?"
- Charts showing fundamental benchmarking gaps.

Clients waiting in the reception area or signing tax returns are repeatedly exposed to the message.

6. Seasonal campaigns

Anchor your benchmarking promotions to moments when clients are most open to improvement:

- Pre–June 30 – urgency around year-end planning.
- July–August – goal-setting for the new financial year.
- November – review before Christmas slowdown.
- February – structure and distribution planning.

7. Sales scripts that reinforce value

Every conversation should hammer home the results benchmarking delivers:

- "Businesses in the top 20% make twice the net profit of the average – we'll show you where you sit."
- "Benchmarking highlights exactly which levers will put another $50,000–$200,000 into your business."

Clients often need to hear this more than once before they take it seriously.

8. Structured follow-ups

Systemise follow-ups every 60–90 days with clients who haven't yet engaged. Contact:

- Compliance-only clients (show them benchmarking is their missing piece).
- Clients who attended a webinar but didn't book a session.
- Past prospects who said "not now."

Repetition plus persistence equals conversion.

The bottom line

Achieving a Top 20% business benchmark is not typically accomplished in a single conversation. It's sold through **consistent education and repeated messaging**. By combining these eight strategies, you keep the benchmarking message at the forefront of the client's mind until they are ready to act.

Educate every client

One of the biggest mistakes accountants make is picking and choosing who they educate. They assume some clients are "too small," "not interested," or "can't afford advisory." That thinking costs practices hundreds of thousands in lost fees.

The truth is simple: **every client should be exposed to benchmarking education.**

Why? Because you never know which client will respond. The quiet client who only comes in for a tax return may turn out to be the one who signs up for quarterly benchmarking reviews worth $1,500 a month. The only way you find out is by educating them.

Consistency builds credibility

When you educate every client, it creates consistency. Your message becomes part of the culture of your practice. Every staff member reinforces it, every client hears it, and over time, it becomes impossible to miss the fact that you provide Top 20% benchmarking services.

Clients don't self-select

Clients don't walk in asking for benchmarking. They don't know what it is or how it works. They only know their problems – low cash flow, high costs, staff issues, and no profit. It's your job to connect those problems to benchmarking. And the only way to do that is to educate them, every time, without exception.

The hidden benefit

Even if a client doesn't act straight away, education plants a seed. That seed grows over time. The client starts to notice your messages, they see the success stories, and eventually, the timing is right. When it is, you've already positioned yourself as the obvious choice.

The bottom line

Benchmarking should never be an exclusive service for a handful of "chosen" clients. Make education universal—every meeting, every email, every newsletter, every client – no exceptions.

Because the one client you don't bother to educate today could be the one who signs up for a $20,000 advisory package tomorrow.

Automate the education process.

If you try to educate every client manually, you'll burn out. That's why most firms fail – they start strong, then stop once they get busy. The answer is simple: **automation**.

Automation takes the hard work out of client education. It ensures every client hears the benchmarking message consistently, whether you remember to send it or not. Once the system is in place, education runs in the background and positions you as the adviser who "never stops delivering value."

Here's how innovative firms do it:

1. Automated email sequences

Build a 12-month drip campaign. Each month, clients get a benchmarking insight, KPI comparison, or success story. One setup – endless delivery. Education that runs while you sleep.

2. CRM triggers and reminders

Use your CRM to do the heavy lifting. Set rules like:

- 60 days after a tax return → send a benchmarking fact sheet.
- 90 days after a client meeting → prompt a follow-up call.

Automation makes sure no one slips through the cracks.

3. Plug-and-play resources

Have benchmarking brochures, one-pagers, and case studies ready to go. Staff should be able to drop them into an email or hand them out in a meeting in seconds. Templates guarantee speed and consistency.

4. TaxFitness tools

The TaxFitness system already gives you fact sheets, reports, and Top 20% comparisons. Automate their delivery – integrate them into your standard client process. Every client gets something, every year.

5. Evergreen video content

Record short, sharp videos that explain Top 20% benchmarking. Host them on your website, email them to clients, and post them on social media. Once created, videos work 24/7 – they educate without you having to repeat yourself 20 times.

The bottom line

Manual education fails because it relies on memory and spare time. Automation never fails. It runs in the background, touches every client, and repeats the benchmarking message until it sticks.

The goal isn't to educate a few clients when you have time. The goal is to **educate every client, all the time, without adding to your workload.**

That's how you scale benchmarking – and that's how you win.

Advanced engagement techniques

Sending emails and newsletters is fine. But if you want clients to act, you need to go beyond the basics. Education alone creates awareness. Engagement creates buy-in.

Advanced engagement is about making benchmarking impossible to ignore. It's not just telling clients what the Top 20% achieve – it's making them feel the gap in their own business and showing them the opportunity that's right in front of them.

Here's how you do it:

1. Tell stories, not statistics

Clients don't remember that "gross margin is 42%." They recall a similar business that increased its gross margin by 5% and earned an additional $180,000 in profit—real-world examples cut through the noise.

2. Ask benchmarking questions

Questions make clients stop and think:

- "What would an extra 10% net profit mean for you?"
- "Do you know how your business compares to the best in your industry?"

When clients answer in their own words, they own the problem – and the solution.

3. Show, don't tell

A chart showing your client below the Top 20% benchmark line is worth more than three pages of explanation. Visuals create instant clarity—and instant motivation to close the gap.

4. Make it a challenge

Turn benchmarking into a competition. Say:

"The top 20% in your industry earn twice the profit. Let's set a goal to beat them."

Business owners love a challenge. Gamification makes improvement exciting, not dull.

5. Use group dynamics

Run small-group workshops where clients see their peers benchmarking their own performance. When they realise other businesses are doing it, they don't want to be left behind. Peer pressure works in your favour.

The bottom line

Education makes clients aware. Engagement makes them act. Use stories, questions, visuals, challenges, and group settings to shift clients from passive listeners to motivated participants.

Because motivated clients don't just understand benchmarking – they buy it, they commit to it, and they pay you for it.

Measuring education effectiveness

Education without measurement is just noise. You can send emails, run webinars, and hand out brochures all day long — but if it doesn't lead to action, it's wasted effort.

The primary purpose of educating clients about benchmarking is to engage them, encourage change, and ultimately drive their payment for advisory services. So, you have to measure if it's working.

1. Are clients engaging?

- Are they opening your emails?
- Are they clicking the benchmarking links?
- Do they show up to webinars and ask questions?

- Are they liking, commenting, or sharing your posts?

If the answer is no, your message isn't cutting through. Change it.

2. Are clients converting?

Education isn't about activity — it's about results. Track:

- How many compliance-only clients start benchmarking reviews?
- How many prospects book a benchmarking session after seeing your material?
- How many clients upgrade from one-off reports to quarterly reviews?

Conversions are the scoreboard.

3. Are clients using your language?

You know education is landing when clients start repeating your own benchmarking phrases back to you:

- "We want to get closer to the top 20%."
- "How do our wages compare to the benchmark?"

That's when you know the seed has been planted.

4. Are fees growing?

At the end of the day, education must show up in your P&L. If benchmarking education is effective, your advisory fees will increase. If fees are flat, the education isn't working.

The bottom line

Don't educate for the sake of it. Educate to get results. Track engagement, track conversions, listen to the language clients use, and measure your fee growth.

If the numbers aren't there, consider changing the message or the delivery method. But never stop educating. In a world full of noise, it's repetition and measurement that turn benchmarking into revenue.

External education and marketing

Educating clients isn't limited to one-on-one meetings. The firms that grow advisory divisions fastest understand that external education doubles as marketing. Every piece of content you push into the market is both a teaching tool and a lead generator.

Webinars and workshops

Running sessions on "How your business stacks up against the Top 20%" or "The five biggest profit drains in small business" positions you as the authority. These events aren't about selling, they're about educating. But education creates demand — clients and prospects quickly want to know how their business compares.

Articles, guides, and reports

Publishing short guides, industry snapshots, or commentary on trends gets attention. A two-page "Top 20% Benchmark Report for Cafés" or "What high-performing tradies do differently" is powerful marketing. It gives away insight, builds credibility, and attracts the right clients.

Digital presence

Social media posts, newsletters, and blogs all serve the same purpose — drip-feeding education into the market. Done consistently, they create a pipeline of clients already primed to value benchmarking before they ever walk through your door.

Media and alliances

Being featured in local press, industry associations, or podcasts multiplies your reach. An accountant who's quoted as a "benchmarking expert" gains authority overnight. Partnerships with software providers, business networks, or advisors extend your educational reach and generate referrals.

The key principle: External education is marketing in disguise. Instead of pushing sales messages, you're teaching business owners how to think about performance, risk, and improvement. That education naturally leads them back to you, the accountant who has the benchmarks, tools, and system to deliver results.

The outcome is straightforward: every external education activity enhances your reputation, fills your pipeline, and transforms benchmarking into the signature service your firm is recognised for.

9

Step 5 - Sell service to client

*'TO SUCCEED, YOU HAVE TO DO SOMETHING
AND BE VERY GOOD AT IT'*
– JOE ROGAN (AMERICAN POSTCAST HOST,
COMEDIAN, 2010S).

You are at STEP 5

Step 1: Systems and practice	Step 2: Information gathering	Step 3: Fees and charging clients
Step 4: Educate clients	**Step 5: Sell service to clients**	Step 6: The two TaxFitness database
Step 7: Select business advisory strategies	Step 8: Top 20% Business Benchmarking Report	Step 9: Advisory meeting (report presentation)
Step 10: Implementing strategies		

The objective of selling benchmarking

The objective of selling benchmarking is not simply to increase fees – it is to deliver meaningful improvement to your clients' businesses while strengthening the value of your own practice.

When you recommend benchmarking, you are not selling another "service." You are offering a **pathway to higher performance, profitability, and peace of mind.** Most business owners are stuck comparing themselves to their own past results or the industry average. That mindset keeps them trapped in mediocrity. By showing them how they measure against the top 20% of businesses in their industry, you reset the standard.

Selling benchmarking is about:

- Shifting client expectations – From "good enough" to "best in class."
- Creating clarity – Turning financial data into actionable insights that clients can use.
- Building confidence – Clients know they are making decisions based on facts, not guesswork.
- Driving accountability – Clients engage more deeply with you when they know there is a measurable gap to close.
- Positioning your practice as essential – You move from being their compliance provider to their strategic advisor.

The result? A win-win outcome. Your clients achieve stronger performance, higher profits, and greater business value. You create deeper, longer-term client relationships and generate new, recurring revenue streams for your practice.

In short, the objective of selling benchmarking is to help clients close the gap between where they are and where the leaders in their industry are—and to make your practice the partner that guides them there.

The right mindset for selling advisory

Selling advisory is not about pushing a service. It's about helping clients achieve outcomes they thought were impossible. Too many accountants approach advisory with the wrong frame of mind—they think clients won't pay, or they fear being seen as "salesy." That mindset will hold you back.

The right mindset is simple: **you are not selling, you are serving.**

Advisory is about creating value, not extracting fees. If your recommendations can save a client $50,000 in wasted costs, or grow their profits by $100,000, then charging them $5,000 for your guidance is not a "cost"—it's a high-return investment. You are giving them clarity, confidence, and direction that they cannot get elsewhere.

When you sell advisory, remember:

- You're the guide, not the vendor. Clients don't want another product—they want leadership and certainty.
- Price follows value. When clients see the size of the gap between where they are now and where they could be, your fee is irrelevant compared to the upside.
- Your role is transformational. Compliance keeps the score. Advisory changes the game.
- Belief is contagious. If you don't believe in the power of benchmarking and advisory, your client never will.

Selling advisory starts in your head. If you see it as optional, your clients will too. If you see it as essential, they'll follow your lead.

The right mindset is knowing that advisory is not about you—it's about giving your clients the insight, direction, and results they deserve.

The TaxFitness selling system

TaxFitness Selling System - Flowchart

Step 1: Understand the Client
- Financial position
- Goals & ambitions

↓

Step 2: Quantify the Gap
- Compare to Top 20%
- Highlight profit gap

↓

Step 3: Demonstrate Value
- Translate insights
- Show financial upside

↓

Step 4: Present the Solution
- Outline advisory plan
- Keep it simple

↓

Step 5: Gain Commitment
- Next step focus
- Emphasise accountability

Selling benchmarking and advisory is not about hard selling—it's about leading clients through a structured conversation that naturally demonstrates value. The system works best when followed step by step:

1. Understand the client
- Clarify their current financial position.
- Identify what matters most to them—their goals, frustrations, and ambitions.
- (See section 6 for details).

2. Quantify the gap
- Show clients how their numbers compare to the Top 20% in their industry.
- Highlight the size of the profit gap in real dollars.
- Make the opportunity tangible, not theoretical.

3. Demonstrate value
- Translate the benchmarking insights into practical strategies.
- Show how closing the gap delivers more profit, cash flow, and business value.
- Position your fee as a small fraction of the upside.

4. Present the solution
- Outline the advisory program clearly (e.g. quarterly reviews, annual benchmarking plan).
- Keep the structure simple and professional—clients want certainty.

5. Gain commitment
- Invite the client to take the next step, not with pressure, but with confidence.
- Emphasise accountability: "Together we can close this gap."

Key Principle
The client is never buying a service—they are buying outcomes. Your role is to connect their current position, the Top 20% benchmark, and the strategies that bridge the gap. When done right, the client will see engaging you as an investment, not a cost.

Quantify the value for every client.

The most potent aspect of selling Top 20% benchmarking is demonstrating to the client, in dollars, what is achievable. Clients don't buy concepts—they buy outcomes. The more you quantify the value, the easier it is for them to see why your service is essential.

When you benchmark a client against the Top 20%, you expose the profit gap: the difference between their current performance and what the best businesses in their industry are achieving. That gap might be in revenue, margins, overheads, or wages efficiency—but when converted into real dollars, it becomes impossible to ignore.

For example:
- A café with $1.2m revenue and net profit of $60k may discover that the Top 20% achieve a 15% net profit margin. That's $180k. The profit gap is $120,000 per year.
- A construction business turning over $10m with 4% net profit ($400k) may find the Top 20% are achieving 8% net profit ($800k). The annual gap is $400,000.

This is not theory—it's a measurable opportunity.

By quantifying value:

- Clients see advisory as an investment, not a cost. Paying you $10,000 to help them close a $200,000 gap is a simple decision
- You eliminate objections. Once the opportunity is framed in dollars, the conversation shifts from "Do I want this?" to "How fast can we start?"
- You drive accountability. The client knows exactly what they are working towards, and every quarterly meeting becomes about progress against that dollar target.

Always remember: **if you can't quantify the value, you can't sell the value.** Every benchmarking conversation should result in a precise, evidence-based calculation of what is possible if the client performs at Top 20% levels.

Your role is not just to show them the gap—it's to lead them in closing it.

Building the client proposal

Forget long reports. Forget complicated documents. The best proposal you can give a client is already built into the TaxFitness system — the one-page Top 20% Benchmarking Summary.

This single page shows their numbers against the best in their industry. It highlights the **profit gap in real dollars** — the difference between their current position and what's possible. That number is the value of your advisory service.

How to use it

1. Print or open the one-page summary (five minutes to prepare).
2. Sit beside the client and walk them through it.

3. Point to the gaps: "Here's where you are… here's where the Top 20% are."
4. Quantify the opportunity: "That's $120,000 per year on the table."
5. Close with confidence: "This is what we'll work on together."

Why it works
- Fast – Always ready in minutes.
- Clear – Clients instantly see the difference.
- Powerful – The dollar gap makes your fee irrelevant.

Key principle: The one-page benchmarking summary is the proposal. It doesn't just explain the value—it proves it.

What benchmarking services can you sell?

The details of each package are outlined in the Pricing chapter. When it comes to selling, your role is not to walk the client through every option—it's to guide them towards the right starting point and then lead them up to the next level when they are ready.

- Start simple – For new clients, the Top 20% Performance Diagnostic Initial benchmarking assessment (one-off) is often the easiest entry point. It's quick to prepare, easy to explain, and shows immediate value by highlighting the profit gap.
- Build momentum – Once a client sees the value, move them into the Top 20% Strategic Performance Review (Annual benchmarking review and 12-month plan). This locks in benchmarking as part of their yearly routine, creating a natural link with tax planning and financial statements.
- Drive accountability – For clients who want real im-provement, the Performance Growth Program (Quarterly benchmarking – minimum 12 months) is where results

happen. Regular reviews keep them focused and account-able, and position you as their ongoing advisor.

- Profit Transformation Program (Monthly benchmarking and advisory implementation – minimum 12-month contract) – Ambitious, growth-focused businesses should be shown the Premium Advisory Membership. This program is about more than benchmarking—it's about building a business that consistently performs at Top 20% levels.

Sales principle

Clients don't buy packages—they buy outcomes. Use the package names confidently, but always frame the conversation around the result: closing the gap, lifting profits, and building a stronger business.

Focus on existing clients first.

When you start selling benchmarking services, the easiest place to begin is not with new prospects—it's with the clients you already have.

Your existing clients already know you, trust you, and value the work you do. You don't need to prove your credibility or explain who you are. What they need is to see how benchmarking can help them achieve better results with the business they already run.

Why start with existing clients?

- Faster wins – You have their financial data on hand, so preparing a benchmarking summary takes minutes.
- Built-in trust – The relationship is already established; you don't have to overcome the barrier of being a stranger.
- Higher conversion rates – Existing clients are far more likely to say yes because they've already experienced your value.

- Lower cost of sales – You don't need to spend time or money chasing new leads.

How to approach it
1. Pick your best-fit clients – Start with businesses where you know benchmarking will uncover clear profit gaps.
2. Run the one-page summary – Prepare the Top 20% Benchmarking Summary in five minutes using their existing data.
3. Book a short meeting – Sit with them, walk through the results, and highlight the profit gap in dollars.
4. Make the offer – Position your benchmarking program as the system to close that gap.

Key principle: Your best opportunities are likely already within your client base. Focus on them first. Benchmarking will deepen relationships, increase fees, and deliver fast results for both you and your clients.

Work the percentages

When selling benchmarking, remember this: you don't need every client to say yes. Success in advisory sales comes from working the percentages.

Why this matters
Many accountants hesitate to offer benchmarking because they fear rejection. The reality is simple: even a modest conversion rate creates a huge impact.

- If you have 100 business clients…
- And only 20% take up benchmarking…
- At $5,000 per year each…
- That's $100,000 in new recurring fees.

You don't need 100%. You need to work the percentages.

How to think about conversion rates
- 10% conversion = advisory is gaining traction, and you're already ahead of most firms.
- 20–30% conversion = you're building a serious advisory practice.
- 50%+ conversion = you've positioned benchmarking as a core service, not an add-on.

How to improve your percentages
- Ask every client – Don't prejudge who will say yes.
- Use the one-page summary – Simple, visual, persuasive.
- Lead with the profit gap – Clients buy outcomes, not reports.
- Track your numbers – Know your own conversion rate and aim to lift it each quarter.

Key principle: Advisory is a percentage game. You don't need every client. You need to consistently offer and show value, and let the percentages work in your favour.

Overcoming common client objectives

Every accountant who sells advisory services will face objections. Don't see objections as rejection—see them as buying signals. When a client pushes back, it means they're thinking seriously about your offer. Your job is to stay calm, confident, and prepared with the correct response.

1. "I can't afford it."
Client meaning: They don't yet see the value outweighing the fee.
Response: "Fair point—but the benchmarking shows a profit gap

of $120,000. Closing even part of that gap makes this service pay for itself many times over. This isn't a cost—it's an investment."

2. "We're already doing okay."
Client meaning: They're comfortable, but haven't considered what's possible.
Response: "Absolutely—you're running a solid business. But the Top 20% in your industry are achieving double the profit margins. Benchmarking shows what's possible when you shift from good to great."

3. "I don't have the time."
Client meaning: They're overwhelmed and fear an extra workload.
Response: "That's exactly why benchmarking works. We break it into simple, practical steps. You get clarity on where to focus so you can save time, not waste it."

4. "I don't need another report."
Client meaning: They've had poor experiences with accountants who give reports without action.
Response: "Agreed—another report by itself won't change anything. That's why our process isn't about reports, it's about accountability. We meet regularly to make sure the strategies get implemented."

5. "I need to think about it."
Client meaning: They're interested but hesitant.
Response: "Of course. Let's schedule a brief follow-up meeting now, so you have time to think, and I can address any questions you may have. That way, momentum isn't lost."

Key principle: Don't argue with objections. Acknowledge, reframe, and refocus on outcomes. Remember: clients don't buy bench-marking—they buy the profit, clarity, and confidence it delivers.

Tracking your sales success

If you don't measure your sales activity, you can't improve it. Just like your clients need benchmarking to track business perfor-mance, you need a simple system to track your own progress in selling benchmarking services.

Why tracking matters

- It shows whether your sales process is working.
- It highlights where you're losing momentum—are clients saying "no" at the proposal stage, or are you failing to generate enough meetings?
- It keeps you motivated. When you see the numbers improve, it builds confidence to keep going.

What to track

Keep it simple—three numbers tell you everything you need:

1. How many client conversations have you had about bench-marking this month?
2. How many one-page summaries have you presented?
3. How many clients have signed up for a benchmarking package?

Setting benchmarks for yourself

- If you talk to 10 clients, aim to present at least eight summaries.
- If you present eight summaries, aim for at least 2–3 con-versions.
- Track your conversion rate: clients who say yes ÷ clients you spoke to.

Even a 20% conversion rate can add tens of thousands in new fees every year.

How to review

At the end of each month, ask yourself:

- How many conversations did I have?
- How many proposals did I present?
- How many clients came on board?
- What's my conversion rate?

Then adjust. If your numbers are low, increase the number of conversations. If you're presenting but not converting, refine how you explain the value.

Key principle: What gets measured gets improved. Track your sales activity and results just as carefully as you track client benchmarks. The numbers will tell you what to improve—and they'll prove that advisory sales success is a system, not luck.

10

Step 6 – From benchmarking to advisory – The two TaxFitness databases

'ACT AS IF WHAT YOU DO MAKES A DIFFERENCE'

– WILLIAM JAMES (AMERICAN PHILOSOPHER, FATHER OF AMERICAN PSYCHOLOGY, LATE 1800S).

You are at STEP 6

Step 1: Systems and practice	Step 2: Information gathering	Step 3: Fees and charging clients
Step 4: Educate clients	Step 5: Sell service to clients	**Step 6: The two TaxFitness databases**
Step 7: Select business advisory strategies	Step 8: Top 20% Business Benchmarking Report	Step 9: Advisory meeting (report presentation)
Step 10: Implementing strategies		

Introduction

Step 6 is the turning point in the Top 20% Business Benchmarking System. Up to this stage, the focus has been on gathering client information, understanding what's important to them, and presenting the benchmarks that reveal the profit gap. Step 6 takes this one step further. It's where you move from diagnosis to prescription — from identifying problems to providing practical solutions.

TaxFitness makes this possible through two separate but connected databases:

1. The Top 20% Business Benchmarking Database – containing over 400 industry benchmarks that compare your client's performance against the best in their field. This database clearly identifies where the client is underperforming and quantifies the gap in both percentage terms and dollar amounts.
2. The Business Advisory Database – containing over 350 practical strategies to improve business performance. These strategies cover every major driver of profitability, including:
   - Increasing sales
   - Reducing cost of goods sold (COGS)
   - Reducing subcontractor costs
   - Reducing wages
   - Reducing rent
   - Reducing overheads
   - Improving the owner's compensation and net profit

The two databases are designed to work hand in hand:
   - The Benchmarking Database identifies where the gap is.
   - The Advisory Database provides proven strategies to close that gap.

This is what transforms benchmarking from just measurement into a complete advisory system. Without strategies, benchmarking is a mirror—it shows the client what's wrong but doesn't help them change. Without benchmarking, strategies are guesswork. Together, they form a structured, evidence-based approach to improving business performance.

Key principle: Step 6 is where accountants stop presenting numbers and start delivering solutions. It's the point where benchmarking becomes advisory—and where fundamental client transformation begins.

The Top 20% business benchmarking database

At the heart of the TaxFitness system is the **Top 20% Business Benchmarking Database**. This database contains over **400 industry benchmarks** covering the full range of Australian small and medium-sized businesses. What makes this database unique is its focus: it measures performance against the **top 20% of businesses**, not the average.

Why the Top 20%?

Industry averages include the weak and the underperforming. They show what's common, not what's possible. By benchmarking against the leaders—the businesses in the top 20%—you reset the standard. Instead of asking, "Are you average?", you ask, "How close are you to the best?"

This shift changes the entire client conversation. Business owners stop focusing on survival and start striving for excellence.

What the database measures

The benchmarking database captures the key drivers of business performance, expressed as percentages of revenue for easy comparison across businesses of any size. Core benchmarks include:

- Revenue
- Cost of Goods Sold (COGS)
- Subcontractor costs
- Wages and labour efficiency
- Rent and occupancy costs
- Overheads
- Owner's compensation
- Net profit

Each of these measures is calculated using industry data and aligned with the performance of the top 20% of businesses in that sector.

How it works in practice

- You enter the client's financial results into the TaxFitness software.
- The database automatically compares their performance against the Top 20%.
- The results are displayed in a one-page benchmarking summary showing:
- The client's actual percentages.
- The Top 20% benchmark.
- The gap between the two, expressed in both % and real dollar terms.

Why this matters for clients

The one-page summary changes the conversation instantly:

- It proves where the business is underperforming.
- It quantifies the opportunity in dollars.
- It gives clients a clear roadmap for where to focus their efforts.

When a client sees that their wages account for 44% of revenue, while the Top 20% run at 36%, and that the difference is costing them $80,000 a year, the value of advisory services becomes undeniable.

Key principle: The benchmarking database serves as a diagnostic tool. It identifies the gaps that are holding a business back and assigns a dollar figure to the opportunity for improvement.

The business advisory database

Benchmarking identifies the problem, but it doesn't solve it. Once you've shown a client the gap between their performance and the Top 20%, the next question is always: "What do I do about it?"

That's where the **TaxFitness Business Advisory Database** comes in.

This database contains over **350 proven strategies** accountants can use to help clients improve performance. Each strategy is practical, actionable, and designed to close the gaps identified through benchmarking.

What the database covers

The strategies are grouped into the major drivers of profitability:

- Increase sales – marketing, pricing, upselling, customer retention, cross-selling.
- Reduce cost of goods sold (COGS) – supplier negotiations, stock management, waste reduction.
- Reduce subcontractor costs – better scheduling, contract terms, replacing subcontractors with staff where viable.
- Reduce wages – rostering efficiency, automation, productivity measures, incentive systems.
- Reduce rent and occupancy costs – lease negotiations, space utilisation, relocation strategies.
- Reduce overheads – energy savings, systems efficiencies, outsourcing non-core tasks.
- Increase net profit and owner's compensation – margin management, pricing models, business model adjustments.

How it works in practice

- Once you identify a gap through benchmarking, you select relevant strategies from the advisory database.
- For example:

- o Benchmark shows subcontractor costs at 25% of revenue vs. 12% in the Top 20%.
- o From the advisory database, you might recommend three strategies: renegotiating subcontractor rates, investing in core staff, and improving project scheduling.
- The client now sees not just the problem, but the pathway to improvement.

Why it matters for clients

Clients are tired of accountants pointing out issues without offering solutions. The Business Advisory Database fixes that problem:

- It provides evidence-based solutions, not vague advice.
- It gives you the tools to turn every benchmarking gap into an action plan.

It positions you as a partner in business improvement—not just a scorekeeper.

Key Principle: Benchmarking reveals where the gaps lie. The advisory database provides instructions on how to close them. Together, they transform you from a compliance accountant to a trusted advisor.

How the two databases work together

The real power of TaxFitness lies in combining the two databases. On their own, each is useful—but when combined, they create a complete, evidence-based advisory system.

The benchmarking database – diagnosis

- Identifies where the client is underperforming.
- Quantifies the gap between actual results and Top 20% performance.

- Converts percentages into real dollar amounts to show the cost of inefficiency.

The advisory database – prescription

- Provides practical strategies tailored to the specific gaps.
- Turns numbers into action by giving the client a clear improvement plan.
- Moves the conversation from "Here's the problem" to "Here's how we fix it."

How it works in practice

1. Run the benchmark – Client's wages are 44% of revenue, while the Top 20% are at 36%.
2. Quantify the gap – On current revenue, that's an $80,000 profit gap.
3. Select strategies – From the advisory database, you choose three targeted actions:
   - o Review rostering to reduce overtime.
   - o Introduce incentive pay linked to productivity.
   - o Automate manual processes with software.
4. Build the plan – Present the one-page summary and recommended strategies as the roadmap to close the gap.

The doctor analogy

Think of it like visiting a doctor:

- Benchmarking is the diagnosis—it shows what's wrong and how serious it is.
- Advisory strategies are the prescription—they provide the treatment plan.
- Used together, they deliver the cure.

Key principle: Benchmarking without strategies is just measurement. Strategies without benchmarking are guesswork.

Together, they create a system that proves the value of your advice and delivers real results for your clients.

Using the databases in practice

Having two world-class databases is only valuable if you know how to use them in a simple, repeatable way. The goal is not to overwhelm clients with data—it's to create a clear pathway from numbers to action.

Step 1: Run the benchmark

- Enter the client's financial results into TaxFitness.
- Generate the one-page Top 20% Benchmarking Summary.
- Highlight the key differences between their results and the Top 20%.

Example: "Your subcontractor costs are 24% of revenue, while the Top 20% operate at 12%."

Step 2: Quantify the gap in dollars

- Convert the percentage difference into a real financial impact.
- This makes the opportunity impossible to ignore.

Example: "On your $5 million turnover, that 12% gap equals $600,000 a year in lost profit."

Step 3: Select advisory strategies

- Go to the Business Advisory Database.
- Search for strategies aligned with the area of weakness.
- Choose 2–3 practical, high-impact strategies to present.

Example: For high subcontractor costs, select strategies such as renegotiating rates, shifting work in-house, and tightening project scheduling.

Step 4: Present to the client
- Sit with the client and show them the one-page summary.
- Point out the gap, explain the dollar impact, and outline the strategies.
- Keep the conversation simple: "Here's where you are. Here's the benchmark. Here's how we close the gap."

Step 5: Build the action plan
- Agree on which strategies to implement first.
- Add accountability by scheduling quarterly or monthly check-ins.
- Use the following benchmarking report to track progress.

Why This Process Works
- Fast – takes minutes, not hours.
- Visual – Clients can see the gaps immediately.
- Action-focused – Every gap leads directly to a solution.
- Repeatable – A system you can use with every client, every year.

Key principle: **Benchmark → Gap → Strategy → Action.**

This is the workflow that turns TaxFitness databases into real-world results.

Positioning with clients

How you explain the databases to clients is just as important as the numbers themselves. Most business owners don't care about "databases" or "systems"—they care about whether you can help them make more money, reduce stress, and build a stronger business. Please keep it simple.

How to position the benchmarking database

Explain it in plain language:

- "We compare your business against the top 20% of performers in your industry."
- "This shows us exactly where you're strong and where you're losing money."
- "The report highlights the profit gap in dollar terms, so you can see what's on the table."

Clients don't need to know how the benchmarks are calculated—they need to trust that the data is credible and relevant.

How to position the advisory database

Frame it as the solution, not a technical tool:

- "Once we know the gaps, we use a database of 350+ strategies to close them."
- "Every strategy is practical and proven—things that real businesses use to improve."
- "This means you're not getting my opinion, you're getting tested solutions matched to your exact challenges."

This shifts the conversation from "I think" to "the system shows," which builds trust and confidence.

How to position the two together

The most powerful positioning line is:

- "Benchmarking shows you where you stand. The advisory strategies show you how to improve. Together, they give us a complete plan to close the profit gap."

This keeps the message clear: it's not about reports, charts, or databases—it's about results.

Key principle: Clients don't buy databases—they buy outcomes. Always position benchmarking and advisory databases as tools that deliver clarity, confidence, and results, rather than as technical features of your software.

Case study – From benchmarking to advisory

Two years ago, an accountant introduced Top 20% benchmarking to a long-term compliance client in the building industry. The client was running a $12 million turnover business with two working directors. On the surface, things appeared fine—but profitability told a different story.

The benchmarking summary revealed:

- Subcontractors at 70% of revenue (Top 20% were at 40%).
- Net profit at $300,000 for two directors—well below industry leaders.
- A clear profit gap of over $1.5 million compared to the Top 20%.

The accountant didn't stop at the numbers. Using the **Business Advisory Database**, they identified strategies to tackle subcontractor costs, improve project scheduling, and bring key trades in-house.

- After 12 months of quarterly benchmarking and advisory sessions, net profit had risen to $756,000.
- After 24 months, profit had grown close to $2 million.

For the client, the change was transformative, resulting in higher profits, increased control, and confidence that they were moving towards industry leadership.

For the accountant, the result was equally powerful: the client transitioned from a $3,000 compliance-only relationship to a $4,000 monthly ($48,000 annual) commitment for ongoing benchmarking and advisory services.

Key principle: This is the system in action. Benchmarking identified the gap. The advisory database provided the strategies. Regular accountability meetings delivered the results.

This is how you move from being a compliance cost to becoming your client's most valuable advisor.

Key principle

The Top 20% Business Benchmarking Database and the Business Advisory Database are powerful on their own—but the real strength comes from using them together.

- Benchmarking without strategies is just measurement. It shows the problem but doesn't provide a solution.
- Strategies without benchmarking are guesswork. They may sound good, but they're not anchored in evidence.

When you combine the two, you create a system that:

1. Proves the opportunity – Benchmarking quantifies the profit gap in precise percentages and dollars.
2. Delivers the solution – Advisory strategies provide practical, proven actions to close that gap.
3. Drives accountability – Each quarter, you re-benchmark, measure progress, and refine the strategies.

This is what makes the TaxFitness approach different. It's not about reports. It's not about theory. It's about turning numbers into results—and positioning you as the advisor who makes it happen.

The principle is simple: Diagnose with benchmarking. Prescribe with strategies. Deliver with accountability.

Chapter summary

Step 6 is the pivot point in the Top 20% Business Benchmarking System. Up until now, you've focused on gathering data and producing the one-page Top 20% Benchmarking Summary. That summary identifies the profit gap, expressed in both percentages and dollars, and proves the opportunity for change.

But clients don't just want to see the problem—they want to know what to do about it. That's why the Business Advisory Database exists. It takes the benchmarking gaps and connects them to practical, proven strategies.

Together, the two databases form a complete system:

1. Benchmarking database → Diagnose the problem and quantify the gap.
2. Advisory database → Prescribe strategies to close the gap.

This is what turns benchmarking from measurement into advisory. Clients get clarity on their current performance and a roadmap for improvement. Accountants move from compliance to trusted advisor.

With Step 6 complete, you are ready for **Step 7: Select Business Advisory Strategies** — where we dive deeper into how to choose the right strategies from the database and build tailored action plans for every client.

11

Step 7 - Select business advisory strategies

'CLARITY ABOUT WHAT MATTERS PROVIDES CLARITY ABOUT WHAT DOES NOT'

– CAL NEWPORTE (HIGHLY INFLUENTIAL FIGURE ON PRODUCTIVITY, FOCUS, AND THE INTERSECTION OF TECHNOLOGY AND WORK, 2022).

You are at STEP 7

Step 1: Systems and practice	Step 2: Information gathering	Step 3: Fees and charging clients
Step 4: Educate clients	Step 5: Sell service to clients	Step 6: The two TaxFitness database
Step 7: Select business advisory strategies	Step 8: Top 20% Business Benchmarking Report	Step 9: Advisory meeting (report presentation)
Step 10: Implementing strategies		

Introduction – Why strategy selection matters

Benchmarking reveals where the gaps lie. But the real value for the client comes from what you do next—choosing the right strategies to close those gaps.

This is where many accountants fall down. They stop at the numbers, leaving clients with a problem but no pathway forward. The result? The client understands the gap but lacks confidence in addressing it. That's not advisory—that's half a service.

Strategy selection is where you turn insight into action. Not every strategy is equal. Some are quick wins, some take time. Some deliver massive impact, others nibble at the edges. The wrong strategy wastes time and money. The right strategy delivers results the client can see and feel.

This is why strategy selection matters:

- It transforms benchmarking from a report into a business improvement system.
- It builds client trust—because you're not just pointing out issues, you're guiding them to solutions.
- It's where your expertise shines. Numbers don't change a business. The right strategies, implemented at the right time, do.

Step 7 is about making strategy selection simple, structured, and repeatable. TaxFitness offers over 350 proven strategies, and our AI helps you match them to your client's specific needs. But in the end, it's your role as the advisor to bring judgment, context, and leadership.

Benchmarking shows the opportunity. Strategy selection turns it into results.

Key steps in strategy selection

Strategy selection doesn't need to be complicated. It's a structured process that takes the results from benchmarking and converts them into a clear action plan for the client. The goal is to move quickly from "here's the gap" to "here's how we close it."

Step 1: Identify the gap

Start with the one-page benchmarking summary.

- Which areas are underperforming compared to the Top 20%?
- Quantify the profit gap in dollars—this becomes the anchor for strategy selection.

Example: Wages at 44% vs 36% = an $80,000 gap.

Step 2: Match the gap to strategy categories
Go to the Business Advisory Database and select the relevant category:
- Increase sales
- Reduce COGS
- Reduce subcontractors
- Reduce wages
- Reduce rent
- Reduce overheads
- Improve net profit/owner's compensation

Example: High subcontractor costs = "Reduce subcontractors" category.

Step 3: Shortlist practical strategies
- From the database, select 2–3 strategies that are:
- Practical for the client's size and resources.
- Likely to deliver meaningful results.
- Easy to explain and understand.

Step 4: Prioritise for impact
Not every strategy is equal. Prioritise by asking:
- Which strategy gives the most significant financial impact?
- Which strategy is most straightforward to implement?
- Which strategy is the client most likely to commit to?

Step 5: Build the action plan
Present the chosen strategies as a simple, step-by-step plan. Keep it clear and achievable:
- "First, we renegotiate your subcontractor agreements."

- "Next, we bring key trades in-house."
- "Then, we introduce better scheduling."

Why this matters

Without a structured process, strategy selection becomes guesswork. With this process, you turn benchmarking insights into an actionable plan the client believes in—and commits to.

Key principle: Always move from numbers to action. Benchmarking shows the profit gap. Strategy selection shows how to close it.

What makes a strategy attractive

When selecting business advisory strategies, accountants must always keep one thing in mind: **our role is to close the gaps revealed by the Top 20% Business Benchmarking process**. Benchmarking highlights where a client is underperforming compared to the best in their industry. Strategy selection is about choosing the most practical and powerful levers to close those gaps.

An attractive strategy is not just one that looks good on paper—it is one that the client will implement, that delivers measurable progress, and that strengthens the client's position against industry benchmarks.

1. Direct link to a benchmarking gap

Attractive strategies are **laser-focused on the gaps that matter most**. If the benchmarking shows staff costs 10% above the top 20%, then strategies around workforce efficiency, rostering, or role design will be attractive because they address the problem head-on. Clients respond when the strategy is tied to a weakness they now see in black and white.

2. Measurable financial impact

A strategy is attractive if the **dollars stack up**. Business owners want clarity: "If I implement this, how much closer will I be to the top 20%? What's the profit improvement?" TaxFitness equips you with the numbers so that you can quantify the return. Clients don't buy ideas—they buy outcomes.

3. Simplicity and speed

The best strategies are **easy to understand and quick to act on**. A complicated restructure may be technically correct, but a simple change to pricing, wastage, or debt collection is often far more attractive because the client can move immediately. Strategies that show results in the next 3–6 months build confidence and momentum.

4. Low resistance, high buy-in

Clients are naturally cautious. An attractive strategy feels achievable with **minimal disruption**. It fits into the way the client already works, or requires only modest changes. Positioning is critical: accountants must frame the strategy as a low-risk, common-sense step that makes the client's life easier, not harder.

5. Alignment with client priorities

Every client has drivers beyond profit. For some, it's **time, stress, lifestyle, or succession**. A strategy becomes more attractive when it solves both the business gap and a personal priority. For example, improving cash flow doesn't just close a benchmark gap—it also means less stress about paying wages every fortnight.

6. Scalable for growth

A desirable strategy doesn't just fix today's weakness—it also **positions the client for future success**. It scales as the business grows. When clients see that the strategy will not only close one gap but also support their expansion, buy-in increases significantly.

Key principle

Attractive strategies are those that **directly close the benchmarking gaps, deliver a clear financial win, and are simple enough for the client to implement with confidence.** As accountants, our job is not to overwhelm clients with every possible strategy, but to select the one or two that hit hardest, prove the value, and build trust. Once clients see the improvement, they'll want more.

The thirteen 'Golden Rules' of strategy selection

The Top 20% Business Benchmarking process shines a spotlight on the gap — where a client's business is underperforming compared to industry leaders. The GAP might be characterised by COGS that are too high, wages that are above benchmark, a low gross margin, overheads that are out of control, or profit margins that are too thin.

The role of the accountant is clear: **select the strategies that close that GAP.** Anything else is a distraction. These thirteen rules ensure that you choose strategies that address the problem directly, resonate with the client's aspirations, and deliver measurable results.

1. Start with the client

Yes, it's about the GAP — but first, understand the **client's financial position and aspirations.** The GAP tells you what to fix, aspirations tell you why it matters. Combine the two.

2. Commercial purpose first

Strategies must have a **genuine purpose to drive business improvement.** If wages are 10% higher than those of the top 20%, the approach could involve rostering, role redesign, or subcontractor reduction. The GAP provides the natural justification.

3. Connect to aspirations
Closing the GAP is non-negotiable — but to secure buy-in, show how fixing it helps achieve the client's **aspirations** (more profit, less stress, time with family, succession).

4. Focus, don't overload
Don't overwhelm the client with too many options. Present **no more than 10 strategies**, each directly tied to the GAP. Advisory is about sharp, targeted action — not long lists.

5. Go after the low-hanging fruit
Pick the strategies that **close the GAP quickly and visibly**. If COGS is too high, start with supplier renegotiation before overhauling the supply chain. Quick wins prove the value of benchmarking.

6. Timing is everything
The GAP won't close itself. Implement early to **maximise benefits**. Every month wages stay too high or debtor days stretch out, the client bleeds profit. Timing is critical.

7. Think long-term
Some GAPs can be closed quickly; others need a staged approach. Attractive strategies create **sustainable, compounding improvements** — not just a one-off band-aid.

8. Balance risk with reward
Closing the GAP must be practical and defensible. Pick strategies that **minimise risk while delivering high returns**. If the GAP is low, gross margin, avoid suggesting a radical restructure when

pricing adjustments or wastage controls can make a significant difference.

9. Use structures smartly
Only introduce structures where they **help close a GAP**. If profit is too low for the risk, a company or trust restructuring may be warranted. If not, keep it simple.

10. Deliver tangible results fast
Clients want to see the GAP closing. Strategies that reduce expenses, enhance cash flow, or increase gross margin convey instant credibility. Put numbers in front of the client: "This will move you 4% closer to the top 20% margin."

11. Combine and layer strategies
Most GAPs aren't closed by a single action. Combine levers. Example: **reduce subcontractors (closing a COGS gap) + improve rostering (closing a wages gap) + price adjustment (lifting gross margin)**. Together, they transform profitability.

12. Keep it simple, keep it defensible
If you can't explain the strategy in plain English and tie it directly back to the GAP, don't recommend it. Simplicity builds confidence, and defensibility ensures compliance.

13. Be ready to refine
Strategy selection is a process. Closing the GAP may take **several drafts of advice, refinement, and recalibration**. Continue refining until the client views it as both achievable and valuable.

☞ **Key principle:** Every strategy must answer one question — **"Does this close the GAP highlighted by benchmarking?"** If the answer is no, it's not the right strategy. The power of advisory lies in relentlessly targeting the GAP, proving progress, and moving the client step by step toward the top 20%.

Manual vs AI strategy selection

Once benchmarking has identified the GAP, the next step is selecting the right strategies to close it. Accountants now have two powerful tools at their disposal: **manual strategy selection** using their professional expertise, and **AI-assisted strategy selection** powered by TaxFitness. Each has its strengths, and the best outcomes come when the two work together.

Manual strategy selection

For decades, accountants have relied on professional judgement and experience to choose strategies. Manual selection involves examining the GAP, weighing the options, and leveraging knowledge of the client's industry, business model, and aspirations.

The strength of manual selection lies in:

- Context and intuition: Accountants can pick up on subtleties AI cannot — client personality, risk appetite, timing, staff capability.
- Relationship building: Clients value advice that feels tailored, not mechanical. Manual selection gives weight to personal insight.
- Experience with similar clients: An accountant who has seen dozens of businesses in the same industry knows what typically works.

But manual selection also has weaknesses: it risks **bias, blind spots, and missed opportunities**. An accountant may default to their "favourite" strategies, overlook alternatives, or fail to see combinations that would close the GAP faster.

AI strategy selection

The TaxFitness database of strategies powers AI selection. The AI analyses the GAP — e.g. wages above benchmark, COGS too high, or profit margins too thin — and instantly suggests the strategies most likely to close it.

The strength of AI selection lies in:

- Breadth of knowledge: AI can draw from hundreds of strategies across industries, far beyond what one accountant can recall.
- Speed and efficiency: The AI instantly highlights the top strategies that match the GAP.
- Combinations and layering: AI sees connections, recommending strategy bundles (e.g. reduce subcontractors + renegotiate suppliers + price adjustments).
- Consistency: Every client, every time, receives strategy options based on the same systematic process.

The weakness of AI selection is that it cannot understand a client's **appetite for change or capacity to implement**. Left unchecked, it may recommend strategies that look perfect on paper but won't work in practice.

The hybrid approach: human expertise + AI

The future of advisory is not accountant vs AI — it's **accountant plus AI**. The AI does the heavy lifting: identifying GAPs, matching them to proven strategies, and suggesting combinations. The accountant adds the human filter: Which strategies best align with the client's aspirations? Which will they implement? Which carry the right balance of risk and reward?

In short:

- AI provides the options.
- The accountant provides the judgment.

Together, they deliver superior strategy selection — fast, targeted, and practical. This hybrid model ensures the accountant is not limited by memory or bias, while also providing strategies that are realistic and achievable for the client sitting in front of them.

Key principle: AI multiplies the accountant's capacity to identify strategies, but it is the accountant's judgement that ensures the right strategies are selected to close the GAP. When combined, the result is more brilliant, faster, and more effective advisory work — moving the client measurably closer to the top 20%.

Human expertise + TaxFitness AI = The superior model

When selecting strategies to close the GAP, the best results don't come from choosing between manual expertise and AI. They come from **combining both.**

AI does the heavy lifting — it takes the GAP, scans the entire strategy database, and instantly suggests proven solutions. It brings speed, consistency, and options that no accountant could recall on their own.

But AI cannot know the client's aspirations, their appetite for change, or the realities of how their business operates. That's where the accountant steps in. Human expertise filters the AI's options, applies professional judgement, and positions the advice in a way that motivates the client to act.

AI provides the options. The accountant provides the wisdom. Together, they close the GAP faster, smarter, and with greater certainty than either could alone.

This is the **superior model**: accountants leveraging AI to expand their capacity, while still leading with their expertise and relationships. It's practical, defensible, and it keeps the accountant at the centre of the advisory process — exactly where clients want them to be.

Case example – Strategy selection in action #1

Benchmarking without action is just theory. The power comes when you identify the GAP and then select practical strategies to close it. Let's look at a real-world case example.

The GAP identified

A building industry client with $12 million turnover and two working directors was benchmarked against the Top 20%. The results showed:

- Subcontractor costs = 70% of revenue (Top 20% benchmark = 40%)
- Net profit = $300,000 (well below benchmark for the risk and effort involved)

This GAP was bleeding the business. The client was effectively working to make subcontractors wealthy while the owners barely received a return.

Manual and AI strategy selection

Using TaxFitness AI, a range of strategies was instantly suggested to address the subcontractor GAP:

- Shift work in-house to reduce subcontractor reliance.
- Introduce apprenticeship and staff training programs.
- Renegotiate supplier and contractor terms.
- Implement tighter project management controls.

The accountant then applied professional judgement. They knew the client aspired to build a sustainable, long-term business and reduce stress from chasing contractors. The AI's options were filtered and prioritised into a staged plan.

The strategies selected

The accountant selected three strategies to implement immediately:

1. Hire skilled employees to replace high-cost subcontractors.
2. Develop apprenticeship programs to build in-house capability and reduce long-term reliance on contractors.
3. Introduce project cost tracking software to monitor labour ratios in real time.

These were chosen because they directly closed the subcontractor GAP, aligned with the client's aspiration of stability, and were achievable in the short term.

Results in practice

- Within 12 months, subcontractor costs dropped from 70% of revenue to 55%.
- Profit grew from $300,000 to $756,000.
- After two years, profit was approaching $2 million, moving the business much closer to Top 20% performance.
- The accountant also benefited, earning $4,000 per month in advisory fees ($48,000 p.a.) for the benchmarking and strategy implementation work.

Key lesson

The benchmarking process identified the GAP. AI produced a list of proven strategies. Human expertise aligned those strategies with the client's aspirations and capacity to implement. The result: **the GAP was closed, the client moved towards the Top 20%, and the accountant delivered measurable value.**

Key principle: Strategy selection is about focus. Don't try to fix everything at once. Target the most significant gap, select the most practical strategies, and prove the results. Success builds momentum — and clients quickly see the value of ongoing advisory services.

Case example – Strategy selection in action #2

The GAP Identified

Jemma Aesthetics Pty Ltd T/A **Skin Societe Karrinyup & Ellenbrook** reported revenue of **$1,050,000 for the year ended 30 June 2024**. Benchmarking against the Top 20% showed the business was strong across wages, overheads, and net profit.

However, one GAP was clear:

- COGS = 30% of revenue (Top 20% benchmark = 25%)

This 5% variance equated to **$52,500 in lost profit** for the year.

Manual and AI strategy selection

TaxFitness AI identified a range of strategies to reduce COGS:

- Renegotiate supplier terms for dermal fillers and injectables.
- Improve stock rotation to reduce expired or wasted products.
- Ensure treatment pricing consistently reflects input cost increases.
- Consolidate suppliers to gain more substantial volume discounts.

The accountant filtered these options through professional judgement. They knew the client aspired to protect profit while maintaining premium product quality and client trust.

The strategies selected

The following three strategies were prioritised and implemented during FY2025:

1. Supplier renegotiation and consolidation – move to preferred supplier contracts with better volume pricing.
2. Inventory control system – implement tighter monitoring and automatic alerts to reduce wastage and expiry.
3. Pricing review – small, transparent treatment price adjustments to ensure rising product costs were passed through.

Results in practice – Achieved by 30 June 2025

Metric	Before (FY2024)	After Strategies (FY2025)	Improvement
Revenue	$1,050,000	$1,050,000	–
COGS %	30%	25%	-5%
COGS $	$315,000	$262,500	-$52,500
Net Profit (improvement only)	–	+$52,500	+17.5% lift in profit

Key lesson

Even high-performing businesses have GAPs. For Skin Societe, a single variance in COGS was silently stripping more than $50,000 in profit every year. The benchmarking process made the GAP visible. AI suggested options. Human expertise ensured that the chosen strategies were practical, defensible, and aligned with the client's aspiration to maintain premium quality.

Key principle: Closing even one GAP can have a significant financial impact. By focusing on the COGS GAP, Skin Societe lifted profit by $52,500 in just 12 months — proving the value of combining AI-driven strategy options with accountant judgment.

Key principle

The power of business advisory doesn't come from clever theory or long lists of ideas. It comes from **focusing on the GAP revealed by benchmarking and selecting strategies that close it.**

Every client has weaknesses compared to the top 20% — higher wages, too fat overheads, too thin margins, and too tight cash flow. The accountant's role is not to overwhelm the client with every possibility, but to **zero in on the one or two gaps that matter most and match them with practical, defensible strategies that the client will implement.**

Advisory success is built on three things:

1. Focus – target the GAP that costs the client the most.
2. Clarity – present strategies in simple, actionable terms.
3. Follow-through – ensure the strategies are implemented and measured.

Clients don't pay for theory. They pay for results. And results only happen when accountants keep strategy selection tied to the GAP, prove progress, and move clients step by step toward the top 20%.

Bottom line: If a strategy doesn't close a GAP, it doesn't belong in the advice.

12.

Step 8 – Top 20% business benchmarking report

'YOU CAN'T IMPROVE WHAT YOU DON'T BENCHMARK'

– W.EDWARD DEMING (AMERICAN STATISTICIAN, PROFESSOR, AUTHOR, AND QUALITY MANAGEMENT CONSULTANT, 1980S).

You are at STEP 8

Step 1: Systems and practice	Step 2: Information gathering	Step 3: Fees and charging clients
Step 4: Educate clients	Step 5: Sell service to clients	Step 6: The two TaxFitness databases
Step 7: Select business advisory strategies	**Step 8: Top 20% Business Benchmarking Report**	Step 9: Advisory meeting (report presentation)
Step 10: Implementing strategies		

Introduction – The role of the report

The Top 20% Business Advisory Report is not just another set of financial figures—it is the turning point where benchmarking transforms into actionable advice. Numbers by themselves don't change a business. What changes a business is when those numbers are translated into insight, framed with context, and backed by a clear roadmap of strategies.

That is the role of the report.

For the client, it provides clarity. It shows them exactly where they stand in comparison to the best operators in their industry.

No more guesswork, no more vague comparisons—just complex data, measured against the top 20%. The report highlights the gaps, but more importantly, it points to the opportunities. It becomes a mirror, showing the client not just where they are today, but where they could be tomorrow if they take the proper steps.

For the accountant, the report is the anchor of the advisory conversation. It's the tool that shifts the meeting from talking about the past to shaping the future. Instead of being seen as a cost or compliance provider, the accountant is positioned as a trusted advisor who delivers measurable value. The report structures the discussion, ensures nothing important is missed, and keeps the focus firmly on what matters most—closing the gap between the client's current performance and the top 20% benchmark.

Every great advisory conversation needs a framework. The Top 20% Business Advisory Report is that framework. It's professional, credible, and easy for clients to understand. It elevates the meeting, drives engagement, and naturally leads into a discussion of practical strategies. Most importantly, it ensures that clients walk away not just with knowledge, but with a clear plan of action and the motivation to implement it.

Purpose of the report

The purpose of the Top 20% Business Advisory Report is simple but powerful: to turn raw data into direction. Clients don't come to us looking for spreadsheets or ratios—they want clarity, certainty, and confidence about what to do next. This report gives them precisely that.

At its core, the report serves three purposes:
1. Clarity through comparison – Clients finally see how their business stacks up against the top 20% in their industry. Not vague rules of thumb, not anecdotal stories, but real benchmarks drawn from the best performers. This gives

them a perspective they can't get anywhere else.

2. Focus on what matters most – Instead of drowning in dozens of numbers, the report identifies the handful of key gaps that matter. It directs attention to the levers that will improve performance and profitability.

3. Catalyst for action – The report is not a destination; it's a starting point. It sets the stage for an advisory conversation that leads to concrete strategies, accountability, and measurable progress. Clients walk away not with theory, but with an action plan tied directly to their numbers and goals.

For accountants, the purpose is equally important. The report elevates your role beyond compliance. It gives structure to your meetings, credibility to your advice, and a consistent way to deliver value that clients immediately recognise. It transforms advisory from something "intangible" into something visual, practical, and outcome-driven.

In short, the report's purpose is to move clients from **uncertainty to clarity, from data to strategy, from discussion to action.** That's what makes it the linchpin of the Top 20% Business Benchmarking System.

Business advisory: with a report vs without a report

A structured report is the difference between delivering advice that inspires action and delivering advice that quickly fades from memory. Clients value what they can see, hold, and revisit. When advice is supported by a clear, professional report, it becomes tangible, credible, and easier to implement. Without a report, advisory conversations risk being seen as informal, less valuable, and easily forgotten.

Business Advisory WITH a Report	Business Advisory WITHOUT a Report
Provides clear documentation, structure, and accountability	No permanent record of advice; discussions are easily lost or misinterpreted
Quantifies improvements in real financial terms (profit, costs, benchmarks)	Benefits are vague and harder for clients to grasp or value
Enhances compliance and audit defence with a documented advisory trail	Higher risk in disputes or challenges due to a lack of documented evidence
Builds client confidence and positions the accountant as a trusted advisor	Perceived as less professional; risks damaging credibility
Justifies premium advisory fees by demonstrating measurable value	Difficult to charge higher-value fees without tangible deliverables
Provides a step-by-step action plan, making strategies easier to implement	Clients may leave meetings unclear, leading to inaction or mistakes
Strengthens client loyalty and generates referrals through a professional process	Missed opportunities to deepen relationships and grow the practice

Bottom line: Advisory without a report is like building a house without plans—it may look like progress in the moment, but it lacks the structure needed for lasting results. A professional report transforms advice from an informal conversation into a high-value service that clients respect, act upon, and are willing to pay premium fees for.

The specific purpose of the Top 20% Business Advisory Report

While many reports in accounting focus on recording the past, the Top 20% Business Advisory Report is different—it is forward-looking and action-oriented. Its specific purpose is to bridge the gap between raw benchmarking data and practical business improvement.

For clients, the report provides:
- A clear performance snapshot – showing exactly how their business measures against the top 20% of their industry.
- Identification of the critical gaps – highlighting the areas that hold back profitability, efficiency, or growth.
- A roadmap of opportunities – outlining the most relevant strategies that will close those gaps and move the business closer to top-tier performance.

For accountants, the report delivers:

- A structured conversation tool – ensuring meetings stay focused on what matters most, not drifting into vague discussion.
- Professional authority – positioning the accountant as a strategic advisor who provides tangible, benchmark-driven insights rather than subjective opinion.
- A pathway to recurring engagement – turning a single report into an ongoing cycle of review, implementation, and measurable improvement.

In essence, the specific purpose of the Top 20% Business Advisory Report is to make benchmarking practical. It transforms complex numbers into a clear story of where the business is now, where it should be, and how to get there. The report ensures that every advisory meeting produces clarity, direction, and commitment—leaving no doubt about the value the accountant provides.

The 10 keys to a superior Top 20% Business Advisory Report

The quality of the report determines the quality of the advisory conversation. An excellent report doesn't just display data — it tells a story, builds trust, and moves clients to action. These 10 keys are what separate an average report from a superior one.

1. Personalised advice – Every strategy must fit the client's situation. No "off the shelf" answers. Clients should feel that this report was specifically written for them.
2. Quantify the value – Show the numbers. Translate recommendations into estimated savings, profit uplift, or cost reductions — strategy by strategy and as a total. Clients believe what they can measure.
3. Logical flow – Structure the report in a clear order: high-

impact strategies first, quick wins up front, longer-term plays last. A logical sequence makes the path forward obvious.

4. A clear, professional report supports clarity – Keep it simple. Avoid jargon. The test is this: can a business owner read it and immediately understand what to do next?

5. Commercial focus – Go beyond tax outcomes. Link every recommendation to a business or commercial benefit — growth, efficiency, or reduced risk. That's what clients care about most.

6. Risk transparency – Give each strategy a simple risk rating (Low, Medium, High). Clients trust advice that acknowledges risks as well as rewards.

7. Actionable steps – Be precise about what needs to be done, by whom, and when. Without actions, reports stay on the shelf. With them, they drive implementation.

8. Professional presentation – Use clear tables, headings, and visuals where helpful. A professional look signals professional advice — and makes the content easy to absorb.

9. Consistency and compliance – Maintain a uniform structure and compliant language across every report. This builds credibility, reduces risk, and makes your process scalable.

10. Executive summary – Open with a one-page overview: key findings, top opportunities, and recommended actions. Busy clients need to see the big picture first.

The result: A superior Top 20% Business Advisory Report isn't just information on paper — it's a roadmap. It motivates clients, strengthens your authority, and justifies premium advisory fees.

Why include and discuss recommendations

Benchmarking without recommendations is like diagnosing a problem without offering a cure. The real value of the Top 20% Business Advisory Report comes from turning insights into clear, practical strategies. Discussing recommendations ensures clients leave the meeting with confidence, clarity, and direction.

What are "recommendations"?

In the context of the Top 20% Business Advisory Report, recommendations are tailored strategies developed for the client. They are not limited to addressing performance gaps against benchmarks — they go much further. Recommendations can cover the full spectrum of tax, business, risk, and wealth matters that affect the client's future.

Examples of recommendations include:

- Structuring – reviewing business or investment structures for tax efficiency, asset protection, and growth.
- Risk management – ensuring appropriate insurances, compliance, and safeguards are in place.
- Asset protection – strengthening legal frameworks to protect personal and business assets.
- Estate planning – putting in place wills, powers of attorney, and succession strategies.
- Wealth creation – developing SMSF strategies, retirement planning, and investment frameworks.
- Business improvement – reducing subcontractor reliance, optimising wage costs, improving margins, or renegotiating leases.
- Tax strategies – maximising available concessions, deductions, and planning opportunities.

In short, recommendations translate benchmarking insights

into a wider advisory conversation — one that looks at the whole client situation, not just their financial performance compared to the Top 20%.

Why recommendations matter

Reason	Description
Holistic advice	Elevates the conversation beyond tax returns by addressing tax, business performance, risk, structuring, and wealth, giving clients the complete picture.
Spot new opportunities	Identifies gaps in planning, structures, risk management, asset protection, insurance, and estate planning — issues that clients may never have considered.
Strengthen compliance	Demonstrates that broader legal, regulatory, and financial risks were reviewed and addressed, protecting both client and advisor.
Differentiate your firm	Position your practice as proactive and strategic, setting you apart from compliance-only firms and deepening client trust.
Grow advisory revenue	Each recommendation opens the door to a project, engagement, or new service — turning insights into recurring income streams.
Protect the advisor	Provides documented evidence that broader risks and opportunities were raised, protecting the advisor from future disputes.
Support long-term retention	Clients stay longer when they consistently see value beyond compliance services — making them more loyal, less price-driven, and more likely to refer others.

Bottom line: Recommendations are where the value lies. They move the report from numbers and benchmarks into a complete advisory framework — covering tax, business, risk, wealth, and succession. By including and discussing recommendations, accountants demonstrate that they are not just compliance providers, but strategic advisors who protect, guide, and grow their clients' wealth.

Structure of the report

The Top 20% Business Advisory Report is built with purpose. Each section is designed to lead the client from context → comparison → position → strategy. The flow is deliberate—so the client can follow the logic and see exactly where value is created.

Here's the structure:

About business advisory

Sets the context. Explains what business advisory is, why it matters, and how this report differs from compliance reporting. Clients immediately see this is about **strategy and improvement**, not just tax.

Industry profile

Provides the benchmark. By showing how the **top 20% of businesses in the industry** perform, the client has a clear standard to measure against. This creates the foundation for the advisory conversation.

Summary – For the Year in Question (e.g., 30 June 2025)

A high-level financial summary of the client's business for the relevant year. This places their numbers in one concise view, so strengths and weaknesses can be identified at a glance.

Business advisory snapshot

Connects the client's data to the benchmarks. This section highlights how they perform against the top 20%, and where the key gaps—and opportunities—exist.

Taxable income

Presents the client's taxable income in a way that ties directly to the advisory. It shows how their current result impacts both cash flow and tax planning, linking compliance to bigger-picture strategy.

Net worth

Expands the focus beyond income. Many business owners lack a clear understanding of their net worth. Including this section positions the accountant as a true advisor who helps clients measure and grow long-term wealth.

Selected business advisory strategies

This is the action section. Tailored strategies are presented, chosen from the TaxFitness advisory database. They target efficiency, profitability, cash flow, risk management, and wealth creation.

Disclaimer

A professional safeguard. It clarifies that the report provides advisory insights but is not a substitute for specialist financial, legal, or investment advice. It protects both the accountant and the client.

The sequence works because it tells a story:

- Start with context.
- Compare to benchmarks.
- Summarise the client's actual year.
- Highlight their gaps.
- Provide strategies to close those gaps.
- Finish with clear professional boundaries.

This structure keeps the report logical, professional, and client-friendly—making the advisory conversation smooth, valuable, and actionable.

Presenting the report to clients

Producing the Top 20% Business Advisory Report is only half the job. The real value is created when the report is presented to the client. A well-prepared report, delivered poorly, will fall flat. A clear, confident presentation turns data into action.

Here's how to make the presentation work:

1. Set the scene

Schedule a dedicated meeting for the report presentation—ideally 60–90 minutes. Position it as a strategic discussion, not a compliance review. Clients need to understand this is about their business future, not just historical numbers.

2. Focus on the story, not the numbers

The client doesn't need every line item explained. What they need is the story:

- How do they compare to the top 20% of their industry?
- Where are they strong?
- Where are the gaps holding them back?
- Numbers support the story—but the conversation should focus on insights and actions.

3. Use visuals to drive engagement

Graphs, charts, and snapshots make it easier for clients to grasp complex information. A simple visual showing the client versus the top 20% is often more powerful than a page of figures.

4. Prioritise key insights

Don't overwhelm the client with 20 points. Highlight the three to five areas that will have the greatest impact. These become the springboard for strategy selection and action planning.

5. Position yourself as the advisor

The report is the tool, but **you are the advisor**. Guide the client through the findings, answer questions, and connect the dots between their current performance and their future potential.

6. Transition to action

Finish the presentation with momentum. Move from "what the

report says" to "what we are going to do." Introduce the advisory strategies you've selected, and frame them as the next logical step.

7. Document outcomes

Agree on action points and record them. This ensures accountability and gives you a clear pathway for follow-up meetings.

The key principle: The report is not the end product. It is a conversation tool. Its purpose is to engage the client, demonstrate the value of benchmarking, and naturally lead into the implementation of business advisory strategies.

Key principle

The **Top 20% Business Advisory Report** is not an end in itself—it's a catalyst for action.

The key principle is simple: **The value of the report is not in the numbers, but in the conversation it creates.**

Clients don't need another document filled with figures. They need clarity, perspective, and direction. The report gives them a structured way to:

- See where they stand compared to the best in their industry.
- Understand the financial impact of their current performance.
- Identify the most significant opportunities for improvement.
- Decide on practical strategies to close the gap.

The accountant's role is not to "deliver a report," but to **guide a strategic discussion.** The report provides the evidence, but you provide the insight, context, and advice.

When presented correctly, the client walks away with:

1. A new understanding of their business position.
2. Clarity on what the top 20% are achieving.
3. Three to five actionable strategies to improve results.

4. Confidence that they are working with a proactive, trusted advisor.

Remember: The report is the tool. The principle is the conversation. The outcome is action.

13.

Step 9 – Advisory meeting (report presentation)

'LEADERSHIP IS HARD TO DEFINE…IF YOU CAN GET PEOPLE TO FOLLOW YOU, YOU'RE A GREAT LEADER'

– INDRA NOOYI (INDIAN BORN AMERICAN BUSINESS LEADER CELEBRATED FOR HER STRATEGIC VISION AND TRANSFORMATIVE LEADERSHIP, CEO OF PEPSI, 2025).

You are at STEP 9

Step 1: Systems and practice	Step 2: Information gathering	Step 3: Fees and charging clients
Step 4: Educate clients	Step 5: Sell service to clients	Step 6: The two TaxFitness databases
Step 7: Select business advisory strategies	Step 8: Top 20% Business Benchmarking Report	**Step 9: Advisory meeting (report presentation)**
Step 10: Implementing strategies		

The objective - purpose

The objective of the advisory meeting is not simply to hand over a report. It is to **create clarity, engagement, and action.**

The Top 20% Business Advisory Report provides the evidence and structure—but the meeting brings it to life. This is where the numbers, benchmarks, and strategies are explained in a way that the client understands and values.

The purpose of the meeting is to:

- Communicate insights clearly – Show the client how their business compares to the top 20% and what that means in real terms.
- Highlight opportunities and risks – Identify the areas where improvement is possible, and where inaction will cost them money, time, or competitive position.
- Position strategies as solutions – Move the client from seeing problems to seeing actionable strategies that can close the gap and build value.
- Demonstrate the accountant's role as advisor – Shift the client's perception from accountant-as-compliance-provider to accountant-as-trusted-strategic-advisor.
- Create commitment – Ensure the client leaves the meeting with clarity on the next steps, and with a sense of accountability to act on the strategies presented.

The key point: The objective of the advisory meeting is not to "report on the past" but to **inspire action for the future**.

When delivered correctly, these meetings strengthen client relationships, lock in ongoing advisory services, and establish the accountant as an indispensable partner in the client's business journey.

The role of advisory meetings in the 10-step system

Advisory meetings are the bridge in the 10-step system. They connect the analysis (Steps 6–8) to the implementation (Step 10). Without this step, the system loses its momentum, and the value of the work completed so far is never fully realised.

By the time you reach Step 9:

- The client's financial information has been gathered and verified.
- Benchmarks have been applied against the top 20% of their industry.

- A business advisory report has been prepared with key insights and selected strategies.

The advisory meeting is where all of this comes together. It transforms raw data and analysis into a **strategic conversation with the client**.

The role of Step 9 is to:
- Present the report in a structured, client-friendly way.
- Interpret the findings so the client understands their position.
- Engage the client in discussing priorities and opportunities.
- Build trust by showing that you are not just reporting numbers—you are guiding decisions.
- Transition from insights to action, setting the stage for Step 10: Implementation.

Think of it this way: Steps 1–8 prepare the ground. Step 9 is where the seeds are planted in the client's mind. Step 10 is where the strategies are implemented and results are achieved.

Without Step 9, the system risks becoming an academic exercise. With Step 9, it becomes a catalyst for real change in the client's business and your role as their advisor.

Structuring advisory meeting for optimal results

Advisory meetings must be structured with a purpose. The objective is not to talk through every page of the report, but to create clarity, engagement, and action. A poorly run meeting risks overwhelming the client or leaving them unsure about next steps. A well-structured meeting positions the accountant as a trusted advisor and ensures the client walks away with confidence and commitment.

1. Prepare, don't wing it
   - Review the client's report thoroughly before the meeting.
   - Highlight the 3–5 most important insights to discuss.
   - Decide in advance which strategies to recommend and how to present them.

2. **Open with context**
   - Begin by explaining the purpose of the meeting: to use benchmarking and advisory insights to improve the client's business performance.
   - Reinforce that this is not compliance work—it's about strategy and results.

3. **Tell the story, not just the numbers**
   - Walk the client through the key findings, showing how they compare to the top 20%.
   - Use plain English and visual aids (graphs, charts, simple ratios).
   - Frame each insight as part of a narrative: "Here's where you are, here's how you compare, and here's why it matters."

4. **Focus on priorities**
   - Don't attempt to cover everything. Highlight the areas with the biggest potential impact.
   - Explain why these issues matter and what the financial upside is if they are addressed.

5. **Introduce strategies as solutions**
   - For each priority, present one or two targeted strategies.
   - Explain the benefit in dollars, risk reduction, or improved efficiency.
   - Keep the focus on outcomes, not technical details.

6. Engage the client

- Ask open questions to involve the client in the discussion.
- Encourage them to reflect: "Does this align with what you've been experiencing?" or "How would it impact your business if we improved this area?"

7. Conclude with clear next steps

- Summarise the key priorities identified.
- Confirm the strategies that will be implemented.
- Schedule the next advisory meeting to maintain accountability.

The principle is simple: Structure creates confidence. When clients see a straightforward process, they take the advice seriously and are more likely to commit. A well-structured meeting transforms the report from a document into a roadmap for action.

The advisory meeting flow

An advisory meeting is not a casual chat. It is a structured, client-focused conversation designed to move from **insight to action**. The report is the tool, but the flow of the meeting determines whether the client leaves with clarity and commitment—or confusion and hesitation.

Below is a proven meeting flow you can follow to achieve optimum results:

1. Opening & positioning (5 minutes)

- Set the purpose: "Today is about understanding your position compared to the top 20% and identifying strategies to help you improve results."
- Reinforce that this is advisory, not compliance.
- Outline the agenda so the client knows what to expect.

2. Industry profile & benchmarks (10 minutes)
- Begin with the industry profile: show what the top 20% are achieving.
- Explain key benchmarks in plain English.
- Position this as the standard your client should be aiming toward.

3. Client summary & snapshot (15 minutes)
- Present the client's results for the year in question.
- Use visuals to show how they compare to the top 20%.
- Focus on 3–5 key differences, not every line item.

Ask questions to engage the client: "Does this align with your experience?"

4. Identify gaps & opportunities (10 minutes)
- Highlight where the business is underperforming compared to the benchmark.
- Quantify the cost of underperformance (e.g., wages 5% higher than top 20% = $85,000).
- Emphasise the upside: what closing the gap could mean in real dollars.

5. Present advisory strategies (15 minutes)
- Introduce 2–3 strategies that directly address the gaps.
- Explain why each strategy was chosen, the potential savings or improvements, and the expected timeframe for results.
- Use the report as evidence, but keep the focus on outcomes and solutions.

6. Agree on Next Steps (5 minutes)
- Confirm which strategies the client wants to pursue first.
- Outline the implementation process (Step 10 in the system).

- Lock in the next meeting or review session to maintain accountability.

7. Closing (5 minutes)
- Summarise the key insights and agreed actions.
- Reinforce the value: "By acting on these strategies, you can reduce costs, improve profitability, and move closer to the top 20% of your industry."
- End on a confident, forward-looking note.

The key principle: The flow keeps the conversation structured and professional. It moves naturally from context → comparison → client position → gaps → strategies → action. When followed consistently, this flow builds client confidence, makes the accountant the trusted advisor, and secures ongoing advisory work.

Positioning the report as a conversational tool

The Top 20% Business Advisory Report is not the product—it is the conversation tool. The value lies not in handing the client a document, but in using that document to guide a structured, engaging discussion that leads to decisions and action.

Too many accountants fall into the trap of "report delivery." They flick through pages, explain numbers, and leave the client with information but no direction. That is not advisory. Advisory means using the report to create clarity, highlight opportunities, and help the client make better business choices.

When positioning the report as a conversation tool:

1. Focus on insights, not pages
The client doesn't need every table explained. They need to understand the story—how they compare to the top 20%, what gaps exist, and what those gaps mean in real terms.

2. Highlight the gaps

The report shows where the business stands in relation to the top performers. Your role is to draw attention to the 2–3 areas that matter most and explain their financial impact.

3. Transition to solutions

Every gap should naturally lead to a strategy. The report is not the end point—it's the bridge to action. Use it to shift the conversation from "here's the problem" to "here's the solution."

4. Keep it visual and client-friendly

Use charts, benchmarks, and simple graphics within the report to drive engagement. Clients respond better to visuals and plain English than dense financial tables.

5. Reinforce professional value

Position the report as evidence of the accountant's expertise. It demonstrates that your advice is grounded in data, comparisons, and structured strategy—not guesswork.

Remember: The report's true purpose is to **start the conversation, build trust, and lead the client into an advisory relationship**. It serves as a door-opener to implementation work, ongoing advisory meetings, and a long-term advisory service model.

Driving engagement – Asking the right questions

Advisory meetings should never be a one-way presentation. If the accountant does all the talking, the client leaves feeling like they've sat through another lecture. The real power comes from **engagement**—getting the client to think, reflect, and talk about their business in a way they rarely do.

The key is asking the right questions. Good questions turn a meeting from information delivery into a collaborative advisory session where the client takes ownership of the insights and strategies.

1. Start with big-picture questions
Open with broad, strategic questions to get the client thinking:
- "What are your biggest challenges in the business right now?"
- "If we could improve just one area over the next 12 months, what would make the biggest difference to you?"
- "Where do you see your business in three years' time?"

2. Use benchmarking to spark reflection
When showing gaps to the top 20%, ask:
- "How does this result feel compared to your day-to-day experience?"
- "Why do you think this gap exists in your business?"
- "What would it mean financially if we could close this gap?"

3. Connect results to goals
Bring the conversation back to personal and business goals:
- "If profitability improved by 10%, what would that allow you to do personally or in the business?"
- "Would reducing subcontractor reliance free up cash flow for growth?"

4. Guide towards strategy commitment
Use questions to move the client from recognition to action:
- "Would you like me to show you some strategies that could close this gap?"
- "Which of these options feels most achievable for you right now?"

- "What's the first step we could take together to make progress?"

5. Avoid yes/no questions

Closed questions shut down engagement. Focus on open questions that begin with "what," "how," or "why." These invite deeper responses and ensure the client is part of the conversation.

Remember: Clients value the opportunity to be heard. The more they talk during the meeting, the more they buy into the strategies. The right questions not only drive engagement—they build trust, strengthen relationships, and increase the likelihood of ongoing advisory work.

Transitioning from insights to strategies

The real value of an advisory meeting comes from helping the client move beyond the numbers. Insights are essential—they highlight how the business is performing and where it falls short compared to the top 20%. But if the meeting stops there, the client is left with awareness, not action.

The role of the advisor is to **bridge the gap between insights and strategies**. This transition is what turns information into improvement.

1. Highlight the gap clearly

Start with a simple statement of fact:

"Your wage costs are 7% higher than the top 20%. That translates into an additional $95,000 a year compared to your competitors."

Quantify the gap in dollars, percentages, or risk—whatever makes the impact real for the client.

2. Emphasise the cost of inaction

Make clear what happens if nothing changes:

"If this continues, over the next three years, this will cost your business nearly $300,000 in lost profit."

This creates urgency and positions the next step as essential, not optional.

3. Introduce the strategy as the solution

Present the recommended strategy as the direct answer to the problem:

"One proven way to bring this back in line is by restructuring rostering and reviewing supplier contracts. This is a strategy we can implement step by step."

4. Keep it practical and client-friendly

Avoid overwhelming the client with too many options.

Focus on two or three strategies that have the most significant impact.

Frame them in plain English: "Here's the problem, here's the solution, here's what it means for you."

5. Gain buy-in through questions

Ask open questions to confirm alignment:

"How do you feel about this recommendation?"

"Would reducing wage costs free up resources for other parts of the business?"

This ensures the client feels part of the decision-making process.

6. Transition smoothly to action

Once agreement is reached, clearly outline the next steps for implementation.

Position this as a partnership: "We'll work with you to roll this out and track the results in your next advisory meeting."

Key principle: Insights show the problem, strategies show the solution. A strong transition connects the two and gives the client confidence that change is both possible and achievable.

Locking in the quarterly or annual service

An advisory meeting should never be a once-off event. The Top 20% Business Advisory Report provides valuable insights, but the true value lies in ongoing review, accountability, and effective **implementation**. To build lasting impact for the client—and generate recurring revenue for the practice—you must secure an annual or quarterly advisory service.

1. Position advisory as a program, not a meeting

Clients must view advisory as a structured service, rather than a one-time conversation. Make it clear that the first meeting is the start of an ongoing journey.

- "Today we've identified key strategies. To make sure these are implemented and monitored, we'll meet quarterly to track results, update benchmarks, and adjust strategies."

2. Show the value of regular reviews

- Explain why annual or quarterly touchpoints are essential:
- Keeps the business accountable to agreed actions.
- Measures progress against the top 20% benchmark.
- Provides an early warning if performance is slipping.
- Creates opportunities to introduce new strategies as the business evolves.

3. Offer a clear service structure
- Quarterly Service – Best for larger or growth-focused clients who want active monitoring and faster improvements.
- Annual Service – Best for stable businesses that still want direction, but with less frequent intervention.

4. Frame it in commercial Terms
Translate the value into dollars:
- "If we can close just one of these gaps, it could add $80,000 to your bottom line. Our annual service ensures you stay on track to achieve that."

5. Use the momentum of the meeting
Don't wait. At the end of the report presentation, schedule the next advisory meeting immediately.
- "Let's book our next review for three months from now so we can measure how these strategies are tracking."

6. Position as part of the relationship
This isn't an upsell—it's professional practice. Business performance can't be transformed in a single session. Clients need ongoing guidance, and accountants need a structure that ensures accountability.

Key principle: Advisory isn't a report—it's a relationship. Locking in annual or quarterly services secures the client's commitment, ensures strategies are implemented, and establishes your practice as a long-term partner in their success.

Managing expectation and boundaries

Advisory meetings create excitement and momentum. Clients identify the gaps, recognise the opportunities, and seek immediate solutions. While this enthusiasm is positive, it also needs to be carefully managed. Without clear expectations and boundaries, advisory meetings can quickly expand beyond their scope, leading to confusion, inefficiency, and frustration for both the accountant and the client.

1. Define the purpose of the meeting

At the start of every advisory session, set the boundaries:

- "Today's focus is on reviewing your performance against the Top 20% benchmarks and identifying strategies for improvement. We won't be going into detailed implementation here—that happens in the next stage."

This frames the meeting as strategic rather than operational.

2. Clarify what the report covers—and what it doesn't

The Top 20% Business Advisory Report offers benchmarking, net worth, taxable income, and selected strategic insights. It is not a tax return, a complete financial plan, or a replacement for specialist advice. Use the disclaimer to reinforce this point and protect both the client and the accountant.

3. Avoid scope creep

Clients often raise unrelated issues during advisory meetings, such as finance broking, legal matters, and HR disputes. Acknowledge the problem, but keep the meeting on track:

- "That's an important issue. Let's note it for follow-up, but today we need to stay focused on the benchmarking results and strategies."

4. Set realistic timeframes

Clients may want all strategies implemented at once. Help them prioritise and pace the work:

- "We've identified six opportunities, but the biggest impact will come from focusing on these two over the next three months. We'll review the rest in future meetings."

5. Reinforce the advisor's role

The accountant is the strategist and guide, not the implementer of every detail. Position yourself as the lead for the process and coordinate specialists as needed.

- "Our role is to benchmark, advise, and guide you. For some strategies, we may involve legal, HR, or finance specialists to assist."

6. Document agreements

Always finish by confirming what was agreed, what will be done, and by whom. This helps avoid misunderstandings and maintains a professional engagement.

Key principle: Advisory meetings must be focused and disciplined. By setting boundaries and managing expectations, you maintain professionalism, protect scope, and ensure clients stay committed to the agreed process.

Follow up and accountability.

An advisory meeting only creates value if the insights and strategies are put into action. Too often, clients leave a meeting motivated, but without structure, the momentum fades, and nothing changes. To ensure results, you must build follow-up and accountability into every advisory service.

1. Document agreed actions

At the close of each meeting, summarise:

- The strategies selected.
- The specific actions to be taken.
- Who is responsible (client, accountant, or external specialist).
- The timeframe for completion.

Provide the client with a written summary or action sheet immediately after the meeting.

2. Lock in the next meeting

Accountability requires regular checkpoints. Before the client leaves, schedule a follow-up review (quarterly or annually). This ensures progress will be measured, not forgotten.

3. Monitor key metrics

Link actions to measurable outcomes—profit improvement, cost reduction, cash flow increases, or net worth growth. At the next meeting, report back on what has changed. This makes progress tangible and keeps the client engaged.

4. Hold the client accountable

It is the client's responsibility to implement many of the strategies. Be firm but supportive:

- "We agreed to review subcontractor contracts. Has that been completed?"
- "If not, what's the barrier, and how can we overcome it before the next review?"

Accountability is part of the value you provide.

5. Provide support between meetings

Offer short check-ins by email or phone if needed, but keep them structured and within the agreed scope. This maintains momentum without letting the service drift into ad-hoc advice.

6. Reinforce wins

At each follow-up, highlight the results achieved since the last meeting. Even minor improvements build client confidence and reinforce the value of ongoing advisory services.

Key principle: Advisory is not about a single conversation—it's about creating continuous improvement. Follow-up and accountability transform recommendations into results, and results into long-term client relationships.

Key principle of advisory meetings

The key principle of advisory meetings is simple: **the purpose is not to present information—it is to create clarity, commitment, and action**.

Advisory meetings are not compliance reviews. They are structured conversations that turn benchmarking insights into agreed strategies. The client doesn't need a page-by-page walk-through of the report—they need to understand what matters, why it matters, and what will be done about it.

When run correctly, advisory meetings:
- Focus the client's attention on the gaps that have the most significant financial impact.
- Translate insights into strategies that the client commits to implementing.
- Establish accountability by locking in follow-up meetings and monitoring progress.

- Reinforce your role as a trusted advisor, not just a compliance provider.

The meeting is the turning point in the 10-step system. Everything that came before (data gathering, benchmarking, report preparation) builds up to this moment. Everything after it (implementation and ongoing service) depends on the commitments made here.

Key principle: The advisory meeting is not about delivering a report—it is about driving decisions. A good meeting leaves the client clear on their position, committed to specific strategies, and accountable for follow-through.

14.

Step 10 – Implementing strategies

'MANAGE THE CAUSE, NOT THE RESULT'

– W.EDWARDS DEMING (MANAGEMENT CONSULTANT
KNOWN AS THE FATHER OF MODERN MANAGEMENT, 1950S).

You are at STEP 10

Step 1: Systems and practice	Step 2: Information gathering	Step 3: Fees and charging clients
Step 4: Educate clients	Step 5: Sell service to clients	Step 6: The two TaxFitness databases
Step 7: Select business advisory strategies	Step 8: Top 20% Business Benchmarking Report	Step 9: Advisory meeting (report presentation)
Step 10: Implementing strategies		

The objective – Purpose of implementation

The real value of advisory work is only realised when strategies are **implemented**. Identifying gaps and recommending solutions is essential, but unless those recommendations are acted upon, nothing changes. The client's business performance remains unchanged, profitability remains flat, and opportunities are wasted.

The objective of this step is simple: **turn advice into action and action into measurable results**.

Implementation ensures:

- Strategies deliver outcomes. A report or meeting without follow-through is just theory. Implementation converts ideas into profit, efficiency, risk reduction, and wealth creation.

- Clients stay accountable. Many business owners know what they should do, but struggle to make it happen. Advisory implementation keeps them focused and on track.
- The advisory relationship deepens. When clients see tangible results from strategies, they stop viewing you as a compliance accountant and start valuing you as a trusted business partner.
- The system comes full circle. The 10-step process begins with gathering data and ends with implementing strategies. This step completes the loop and sets up the next cycle of benchmarking, reporting, and improvement.

Key principle: The purpose of implementation is not just to advise the client—it is to create change in the business. Without this step, even the best insights remain unused potential. With it, the accountant proves their value, and the client experiences real, measurable improvement.

The role of the accountant in implementation

Implementation is where strategy turns into results. The benchmarking report identifies performance gaps and highlights the strategies most likely to close them — but unless those strategies are implemented, nothing changes in the client's business. This is where the accountant's role is critical.

1. Turning insight into action

Clients often struggle to move from understanding the problem to fixing it. They may agree that wages are too high, or that margins are too thin, but day-to-day demands push longer-term improvements to the background. The accountant's role is to bridge this gap — taking the insights from benchmarking and guiding the client into concrete, scheduled actions.

2. Accountability partner
One of the most significant values an accountant can bring is the ability to hold others accountable. By setting clear expectations, timelines, and scheduling follow-up meetings, the accountant ensures that strategies are not just on paper. When clients know they'll be reporting progress back to their advisor, implementation rates increase dramatically.

3. Facilitator of resources
Accountants don't have to do all the work themselves. Instead, they act as the facilitator — connecting clients with the right people, tools, or training. For example:
- If subcontractor costs are too high, the accountant may introduce a cost-control specialist.
- If pricing is inconsistent, they may recommend software tools or pricing models.
- If cash flow is weak, they may arrange a session with a finance broker or banker.
- The accountant becomes the hub that directs the client to the right resources.

4. Monitoring and measuring progress
Implementation is never a one-off. Every strategy needs to be tracked against key performance indicators. The accountant helps set the metrics, monitors the numbers, and compares progress back to the Top 20% benchmarks. This creates an ongoing cycle of improvement.

5. Maintaining realism and focus

Clients may want to implement too many changes at once or chase unrealistic outcomes. The accountant brings objectivity and focus. By prioritising the two or three strategies with the highest leverage, they prevent overwhelm and ensure momentum is maintained.

Key principle: The accountant's role in implementation is not about doing the work inside the client's business. It is about **guiding, facilitating, and holding the client accountable** so that the chosen strategies are executed effectively. The benchmarking process provides direction, which the accountant ensures is followed through to results.

From strategy selection to action plan

Selecting the right strategies is only the halfway point. The actual value lies in converting those strategies into a clear, practical action plan that the client can commit to and follow. Without this step, even the best strategy remains just a good idea.

1. Prioritise the right strategies

After benchmarking and strategy selection, the accountant and client must agree on what to focus on first. Not every gap can or should be tackled immediately. The aim is to identify the strategies with:

- The highest financial impact (profit, cash flow, or efficiency gains).
- The quickest wins to build momentum.
- The best alignment with the client's goals and capacity.

2. Break strategies into clear actions

Each chosen strategy must be broken down into practical, step-by-step tasks. For example, "reduce subcontractor costs" becomes:

1. Review current subcontractor agreements.
2. Benchmark rates against industry averages.
3. Negotiate new terms or source alternative suppliers.
4. Monitor savings monthly.

This clarity ensures that strategies move beyond concepts and into manageable actions.

3. Assign responsibilities

Every action needs an owner. The accountant helps the client determine **who** in the business will be responsible for each task. Where the client lacks internal capacity, the accountant can recommend external advisors, consultants, or software solutions.

4. Set timelines and milestones

An action plan without deadlines is unlikely to succeed. The accountant guides the client in setting realistic but firm timeframes:

- Immediate (next 30 days).
- Medium term (3–6 months).
- Long term (6–12 months).

Milestones should align with quarterly or annual advisory meetings, ensuring progress is reviewed.

5. Document the plan

The accountant's role is to document the agreed actions into a simple, structured plan that the client can follow. This becomes the roadmap — a working document that guides both day-to-day business improvement and future advisory sessions.

Key principle: The bridge between strategy and implementation is the action plan. Accountants create accountability, clarity, and structure by helping clients move from identifying strategies to committing to defined actions, responsibilities, and timelines.

Client commitment and buy-in

No strategy, no matter how well designed, will deliver results unless the client is committed to implementing it. Accountants can provide the insight, the benchmarks, and the roadmap — but true progress depends on the client taking ownership. The most effective advisory relationships are built on genuine commitment and buy-in from the business owner and their team.

1. The client must own the outcomes

The accountant's role is to guide and facilitate, but the client must accept responsibility for execution. This starts with making it clear that the strategies belong to the client — not the accountant. When clients see the link between the strategies and their own goals (profit growth, reduced stress, improved lifestyle), they are far more likely to follow through.

2. Engage emotion as well as logic

Clients don't commit solely based on numbers. They commit because they can picture what the results will mean for them — more profit, more freedom, less risk. Accountants should connect each strategy back to the client's drivers. For example:

- "This strategy will add $80,000 to your bottom line — which is the extra cash flow you said you wanted to fund staff bonuses and reduce your workload."

3. Secure agreement in the meeting

At the advisory meeting, don't move past the action plan until the client verbally agrees:

- Which strategies will they commit to?

- Who in their team will be responsible?
- When the actions will be completed.

Without explicit commitment in the room, strategies are likely to be delayed or ignored once daily pressures return.

4. Build accountability structures

Commitment is reinforced by accountability. Setting quarterly or monthly follow-up meetings ensures the client knows they will be reporting back on progress. Documenting agreed actions and timelines in the benchmarking report or an action sheet creates a visible reminder of what they promised to achieve.

5. Celebrate wins and progress

Client buy-in strengthens when they see results. Celebrating even small wins — such as a cost savings, a successful system improvement, or a profitable month — reinforces their commitment and builds momentum for further change.

Key principle: Without client commitment, even the best advisory advice remains unused. The accountant's role is to secure buy-in, link strategies to personal goals, and establish accountability so that improvement becomes inevitable.

Creating the implementation plan

Once strategies have been prioritised and the client has committed to action, the next step is to build a practical implementation plan. This plan is the working document that transforms ideas into specific, measurable, and achievable outcomes. It provides clarity for the client and holds both the client and the accountant accountable.

1. Translate strategies into actions

Each selected strategy must be broken down into **clear, actionable steps**. For example, if the strategy is "improve debtor collection", the action plan might include:

1. Review current debtor days and ageing reports.
2. Introduce debtor management software.
3. Implement automated reminders.
4. Allocate responsibility to the admin staff for weekly follow-up.

Breaking strategies into steps removes ambiguity and ensures progress can be measured.

2. Assign responsibilities

Every action needs a **named person** responsible for completion. This could be the business owner, a key staff member, or an external specialist. The accountant's role is to help the client assign the right tasks to the right people — ensuring accountability is unambiguous.

3. Set timelines and deadlines

An action without a deadline is unlikely to be completed on time. The implementation plan should set firm timeframes:

- Immediate (within 30 days).
- Short term (3 months).
- Medium term (6 months).
- Long term (12 months).

These timeframes should align with advisory meeting cycles, allowing for progress to be regularly reviewed.

4. Define success measures

Each action should include a method for measuring success. This may be financial (profit uplift, cost reduction), operational (time saved, errors reduced), or behavioural (new processes followed). Clear success measures keep the client focused and demonstrate tangible results.

5. Document the plan

The accountant should prepare a concise, one-page implementation plan with the following columns:

- Strategy selected.
- Key actions.
- Responsible person.
- Deadline.
- Success measure.
- Progress notes.

This document becomes the client's roadmap — easy to follow, easy to update, and always accessible.

6. Integrate accountability

Finally, the plan should build in **regular checkpoints**. This could be a quarterly advisory meeting, monthly coaching calls, or progress updates logged by the client. These checkpoints turn the plan from a static document into a living tool for improvement.

Key principle: A well-structured implementation plan turns insight into momentum. By documenting clear actions, responsibilities, and timelines, accountants ensure that strategies are not just understood but acted upon.

Tracking progress and measuring outcomes

It's not enough to recommend a strategy and tick the box. Real change occurs when we measure whether the plan is being implemented and assess its impact on the client's business. If we don't track and measure, then all we've done is provide ideas; we haven't actually achieved anything. Clients don't pay us for ideas — they pay us for results.

1. Set clear metrics

Every strategy requires a specific target or goal to be attached to it. If it's about wages, we measure wages as a % of revenue. If it's debtor control, we measure debtor days. If it's profitability, we measure net profit as a percentage of revenue. Without a number, you can't prove improvement.

2. Build accountability into the plan

The best way to keep clients moving forward is to check in regularly. That means setting review points:

- Monthly for urgent or high-impact strategies.
- Quarterly for medium-term projects.
- Annually for the big-picture outcomes.

When clients know they'll be reporting back, implementation rates skyrocket.

3. Benchmark the results

Clients understand progress best when you show them how they compare to the Top 20%. For example:

- "Last year, your subcontractor costs were 70% of revenue. After implementing the strategy, they're now down to 55%. The Top 20% operate at 40%. We're not there yet, but we've closed the gap by 15%."

That's powerful. It shows momentum and makes the value of our advice crystal clear.

4. Keep it simple and visible
Document progress in plain English. Use one-page action plans, KPI dashboards, or summary reports. The goal is to make results obvious, not to bury them in technical detail.

5. Adjust when needed
Not every strategy hits the mark straight away. If the numbers aren't moving, then revisit the plan, tweak the approach, or replace the strategy with one that will deliver better results. Clients respect honesty and adaptability.

Key principle: What gets measured gets improved. Our role as accountants is to ensure that strategies are not only discussed but also implemented, tracked, and delivered upon. When we measure progress and keep clients accountable, results follow.

Managing barriers and resistance

Every strategy looks good on paper. The numbers stack up, the benefits are clear, and the path forward makes sense. But the real world is messy. Staff resist change, systems don't always cooperate, and business owners often revert to old habits. If you're serious about delivering outcomes, you need to manage the barriers and resistance head-on.

Call out the barriers early.
Barriers usually fall into three buckets:
- Practical – not enough cash, not enough time, not enough people.
- Knowledge – the client doesn't fully understand what to do

or how to do it.
- Emotional – fear of risk, fear of losing control, or the classic "we've always done it this way."

Your job is to name it. Once the barrier is on the table, it stops being an excuse and becomes a problem to solve.

Don't ignore resistance.

When a client pushes back, it doesn't always mean no. It's often a signal they need reassurance. Acknowledge the concern, show you've heard it, and then get back to the facts. For example: "Yes, staff will grumble about changing rosters. That's natural. But here's the upside — it saves $40,000 a year, and we can reinvest part of that in training and communication."

Break it down

Significant changes overwhelm people. The solution is straight-forward: break the strategy into manageable, small steps. Help the client focus on one change, one quick win at a time. Momentum builds, fear drops, and before they know it, the bigger strategy is in place.

Reframe the story

Resistance is usually about loss — more cost, more effort, more disruption. Flip the narrative to focus on gain — higher profit, less stress, more security. "This isn't about spending $5,000. It's about making $25,000." When you shift the story, the resistance starts to fade.

Hold them accountable

Sometimes resistance is just inertia. Clients nod in the meeting, then do nothing. This is where accountability matters. Remind them of their commitments, measure progress, and follow up. Be firm but supportive. Progress breeds confidence, and confidence drives change.

Key principle: Resistance is normal, but it's not fatal. If you can circumvent the barriers, validate the concerns, and keep the client focused on outcomes, you'll turn hesitation into action. This is where accountants move from being advisors on paper to change-makers in practice.

Common barriers and how to respond

Barrier 1: "I don't have the cash flow to do this."
- Response: "That's exactly why we need this strategy. The numbers show you'll free up $60,000 in 12 months. Let's stage the change so the business funds itself."

Barrier 2: "My staff won't accept it."
- Response: "Staff always resist change at first. The key is communication. Let's show them how this improves stability and creates room for wage growth and training. Resistance drops once they see the upside."

Barrier 3: "I don't have the time."
- Response: "Time isn't the issue — priorities are. We're talking about two hours a week for a $40,000 return. That's not a time cost, that's an investment."

Barrier 4: "We've always done it this way."
- Response: "And that's why the results are the same every year. If you want Top 20% outcomes, you can't run on the bottom 80% systems. Doing nothing guarantees no improvement."

Barrier 5: "I don't fully understand how it works."
- Response: "That's our job. We'll break it down step by step, handle the technical side, and keep you focused on the big picture — profit, cash, and growth."

Barrier 6: "I'm worried about the risk."
- Response: "Risk isn't eliminated by standing still. Doing nothing is its own risk — missed profit, wasted expenses, and competitive decline. The numbers tell us this is a managed risk with a clear return."

Key takeaway: Every barrier is a doorway. If you listen, reframe, and refocus the conversation on outcomes, resistance can turn into commitment.

Celebrating wins and reinforcing value

Implementation is not just about ticking boxes — it's about building momentum. Every time a client achieves a result, no matter how small, it reinforces that the process works and that their investment in advisory services is paying off. If you want clients to stay engaged, committed, and excited about future strategies, you must celebrate their wins and constantly reinforce the value of the work being done.

Acknowledge progress early

Don't wait until the entire strategy is complete. Recognise the first milestone, the first improvement in numbers, the first successful staff change. A business owner who sees early results is far more likely to keep pushing through the more complicated steps.

Make the results tangible.

Translate outcomes into dollars, percentages, or clear performance measures. Don't just say, "That's going well." Say, "This change has already added $15,000 to your bottom line in three months." When you tie actions to measurable gains, the value is undeniable.

Celebrate in a way that motivates
Celebration doesn't have to mean balloons and champagne. It means taking a moment to pause and acknowledge progress. For some clients, that's a congratulatory email with the numbers highlighted. For others, it's a quick note in the meeting, "Well done — you've hit the target." The key is to reinforce that their effort produced results.

Reinforce the advisory value.
Always link the win back to the advisory process:
- "This is the result of us working through benchmarking and strategy selection."
- "Without making that change, this money would still be leaking out of the business."
- "This shows the value of keeping you on track each quarter."

Clients need to see that the progress isn't accidental — it's the product of structured advice and accountability.

Use wins to fuel momentum.
Each success builds credibility and confidence, both in you as the advisor and in the process itself. Use wins as a platform to tackle the following strategy: "Now that we've added $20,000 profit here, let's apply the same discipline to this next area." Success breeds success.

Key principle: Wins build belief. By celebrating progress and linking it directly to your advisory process, you not only keep clients motivated but also solidify the perception of value that underpins long-term relationships and recurring advisory revenue.

Key principle of implementation

Strategies only create value when they are implemented. A brilliant report sitting in a drawer is worth nothing. The key principle of implementation is simple: **move from talk to action, and from action to measurable results**.

Implementation is about discipline, not inspiration. Clients rarely fail because the strategy was wrong — they fail because they didn't follow through. The accountant's role is to bridge that gap. We provide structure, accountability, and focus to ensure that what was agreed upon in the meeting is actually implemented in the business.

Every strategy must be:
- Clear – broken into specific steps with who, what, and when defined.
- Measured – tracked with numbers that show progress and results.
- Reviewed – checked regularly to keep the client accountable.
- Adjusted – fine-tuned as barriers arise or circumstances change.

The principle is not perfection; it is progress: small wins, consistently achieved, compound into significant results. The accountant's steady hand ensures clients stay on track, overcome resistance, and experience the benefits of moving into the Top 20%.

Key principle: Implementation is the bridge between strategy and results. Without it, benchmarking and planning are just theory. With it, clients achieve real gains in profit, cash flow, and business performance — and that's the value they will never forget.

15.

Risk management and professional standards

'IF YOU DON'T KNOW WHERE YOU ARE GOING, YOU MIGHT WIND UP SOMEWHERE ELSE'

– YOGI BERRA (FAMOUS AMERICAN BASEBALL CATCHER AND COACH, 1950S).

Introduction – why risk management matters

Advisory work is powerful. Benchmarking and strategy implementation can transform a business — but with that opportunity comes responsibility. As accountants, we are trusted with more than numbers. We are trusted with decisions that impact livelihoods, wealth, and futures. That trust brings risk, and managing that risk is as important as delivering the advice itself.

In the compliance world, risk is primarily managed through rules and reporting standards. In the advisory world, the risk is more subtle. It comes from how advice is presented, how outcomes are communicated, and whether the accountant has set clear boundaries. A strategy that delivers outstanding results for one client may create issues for another if the context, assumptions, and limitations aren't adequately explained and documented.

Risk management is not about being pessimistic or cautious to the point of inaction. It is about being professional, structured, and prepared. When we manage risk effectively, we protect the client, safeguard ourselves, and enhance the credibility of our advisory services. Clients respect advisors who are both ambitious in their strategies and disciplined in their professionalism.

The key principle is simple: **great advice is worthless if it puts the accountant or the client at risk**. Every recommendation must sit on a foundation of professional standards, clear documentation, and ethical practice. Get this right, and you not only keep everything legal — you elevate the standing of your firm and strengthen client trust.

Legal obligations in advisory

When accountants move into benchmarking and advisory, the rules don't disappear — they tighten. Every piece of advice must be delivered within the framework of Australian law and the professional standards that govern us. Failing to fulfil these obligations is not only unprofessional but can also expose both the client and the accountant to serious consequences.

The Tax Agent Services Act (TASA)

If you are registered as a tax agent, you are bound by the Code of Professional Conduct under the Tax Agent Services Act. This includes obligations to:

- Act honestly and with integrity.
- Comply with taxation laws in the conduct of your practice.
- Maintain professional competence in all services you provide.
- Take reasonable care to ensure tax advice is correct and supported.

When benchmarking leads to strategies that impact a client's tax position, you must ensure the advice is consistent with your registration obligations.

Corporations Act & Financial Services Law

Benchmarking and business advisory services frequently address areas such as finance, superannuation, and investments. If your recommendations involve financial product advice, you may enter regulated territory under the Corporations Act and require an Australian Financial Services Licence (AFSL). Knowing where accounting advisory ends and financial advice begins is critical. The safe position: if the strategy involves recommending a specific financial product (e.g. superannuation fund, insurance policy, managed investment), refer to a licensed adviser.

Fair Work & employment law

Advisory strategies sometimes involve wages, rostering, or staffing models. While accountants can advise on numbers, cost structures, and compliance implications, you must not stray into areas that require legal advice under the Fair Work Act. Again, the professional approach is to highlight the opportunity and, if needed, refer the client to an employment law specialist.

Privacy and data security

By gathering benchmarking data, accountants collect sensitive business information. The Privacy Act and client confidentiality obligations apply. Advisory services must adhere to the same data security standards as compliance work, including robust IT protections, confidentiality agreements, and secure storage.

The ATO and record-peeping obligations

When strategies affect tax outcomes, the ATO expects documentation that shows reasonable care was taken in forming the advice. Every recommendation must be backed by calculations, assumptions, and records that can be produced if ever questioned.

Key principle: Advisory work doesn't exempt you from legal obligations — it extends them. As accountants, we must know our boundaries, document carefully, and when in doubt, refer to a licensed professional. Staying within the law is not just about compliance, it's about safeguarding the trust clients place in us.

Professional and ethical standards

Advisory isn't a free-for-all. The same standards that govern your compliance work apply to benchmarking and strategy advice — and in some areas, the bar is higher. Clients trust us with decisions that affect profit, cash flow, staff and risk. That trust must sit on a foundation of professional ethics and disciplined practice.

The core standards that apply

- APES 110 – Code of Ethics for Professional Accountants

  The five fundamentals: **Integrity, Objectivity, Professional Competence & Due Care, Confidentiality, Professional Behaviour**. Apply them to every engagement, meeting and recommendation.

- APES 220 – Taxation Services

  Reasonable care, not being associated with false/misleading statements, documenting assumptions, and explaining uncertainties in tax outcomes.

- APES 305 – Terms of Engagement

  Clear scope, responsibilities, limitations, fees, and timing. No advisory without a written engagement.

- APES 325 – Risk Management for Firms (and APES 320 – Quality Management if applicable)

Policies, procedures, reviews and documentation that keep advice consistent, accurate and defensible.

- APES 225 – Valuation Services (if you include valuations)

  Objectivity, basis of value, assumptions, and disclosure requirements.

Bottom line: Every advisory recommendation must be ethical, within the scope of competence, clearly scoped, thoroughly documented, and supported by evidence.

Threats to compliance — and how to safeguard

APES 110 identifies common threats. In advisory, they show up like this:

- Self-interest: Success fees, referral commissions, or selling related services/tools.

  Safeguards: Full disclosure in writing, client consent, avoid contingent fees where prohibited or where they create undue pressure, separate pricing decisions from advice, and independent review if needed.

- Self-review: Advising on a system or structure you implemented and then "reviewing" your own work.

  Safeguards: Peer review, clear separation of roles, and disclosure of any potential conflicts.

- Advocacy: Over-selling a strategy or making claims that sound like guarantees.

  Safeguards: Balanced wording, evidence-based projections, include assumptions and ranges, no promises of outcomes.

- Familiarity: Long-standing client relationships dulling scepticism.

  Safeguards: Rotate reviewers, use checklists, and require second-partner sign-off on major advice.

- Intimidation: Client pressure to "make the numbers work."

  Safeguards: Document pushback, stick to the facts, escalate or disengage if necessary.

Competence and due care (no guesswork)
- Only advise where you are competent. If the strategy involves legal, financial, HR, or workplace law, refer to a licensed/specialist adviser.
- Keep CPD current for benchmarking, pricing, tax, and sector knowledge.
- Use conservative assumptions, show ranges, and label estimates clearly.

Independence & conflicts
- Independence may not be required for non-assurance advisory, but objectivity is non-negotiable.
- Disclose referral relationships (e.g., finance solutions, software partners) and obtain informed consent before proceeding.
- Where a material conflict can't be managed with safeguards, don't act.

Confidentiality & privacy
- Treat benchmarking data like you treat tax data: strict confidentiality.
- Use secure systems, access controls, and client consent for any third-party sharing (portals, finance providers, integrations).

- Never use client data in marketing or case studies without express written permission and anonymisation where required.

Professional behaviour in communications
- Be truthful and not misleading in proposals, reports and marketing.
- Translate results into dollars and KPIs, but avoid guarantees.
- Every chart/table must have sources, assumptions, dates and rule years.

NOCLAR (Non-Compliance with Laws and Regulations)
- If advisory uncovers wage underpayments, cash skimming, tax evasion or similar, follow the NOCLAR response: raise internally with the client, assess the public interest, and take further action as required by the Code and law. Document every step.

Engagement & documentation essentials
- Written engagement specific to advisory/benchmarking (APES 305).
- Scope & limitations: what's included/excluded; reliance on client-provided data; assumptions; no audit assurance.
- Working papers: inputs, calculations, sources, versions; keep them orderly and reproducible.
- Management sign-off: client acknowledges assumptions, responsibilities and decisions.

Key principle: Professional ethics are not paperwork — they're the backbone of advisory. When you act with integrity, objectivity, competence and discipline, you protect the client, protect the firm, and strengthen the value of your benchmarking service.

Defining scope and boundaries

Advisory fails when expectations are vague. Scope creep is the fastest way to create risk, write-offs, and unhappy clients. Your job is to **define precisely what's included, what's excluded, who does what, and how changes get approved** — before any work starts.

What's in scope (for Top 20% Benchmarking & Advisory)

- Data review & benchmarking: Analyse client-supplied figures; compare to Top 20% KPIs; identify gaps/opportunities.
- Strategy recommendations: Prioritised actions to improve profit, cash flow, efficiency, pricing, costs and risk.
- Action plan & timelines: Who/what/when with measurable targets.
- Progress reviews: Monthly/quarterly check-ins; update scorecards; adjust as needed.
- Documentation: Meeting notes, assumptions, calculations, and a written advisory report.

What's explicitly out of scope (unless separately engaged)

- Financial product advice (Corporations Act/AFSL territory).
- Legal advice (contracts, leases, HR law, company/trust deeds).
- Tax opinions beyond ordinary compliance or agreed advice scope.
- Valuations requiring APES 225 compliance (unless separately engaged).
- Audit/assurance on data provided by the client.
- Systems implementation (software configuration, payroll changes, POS rebuild) beyond agreed guidance.
- Recruitment/HR management beyond structural cost advice.

Boundary rule: If it needs a licence (AFSL), a practising certificate beyond your scope, or a lawyer/HR specialist—refer, don't improvise.

Responsibilities: client vs accountant

The client provides: complete and accurate data, access to systems, staff time for implementation, and decisions and approvals.

The accountant provides Benchmarking analysis, advice and options, financial modelling, implementation plans, progress reviews, and referrals to specialists as needed.

Assumptions & data reliance

- Advice relies on client-supplied information, which is not audited.
- Results depend on timely implementation by the client and external factors beyond our control (market, staff, suppliers).
- Calculations are prepared using stated rule-year settings and published thresholds at the report date.

Scope control (how to prevent creep)

- Single point of truth: One written Engagement & Scope Summary (1–2 pages) attached to the proposal.
- Change control: Any new tasks/requests are logged, priced, and approved before work starts.
- Timeboxing: Reviews are limited to defined sessions (e.g., 60–90 minutes) with a pre-set agenda.
- Issue register: Barriers, decisions, and scope changes captured in writing after each meeting.

Sample scope clause (use/adapt)

Scope of services: We will analyse your FY2025 management accounts and KPI history, benchmark against the TaxFitness Top 20% standards for your industry, and provide written recommendations with an implementation plan. We will meet quarterly to review progress and update the plan.

Exclusions: This engagement does not include financial product advice, legal advice, HR law advice, audit/assurance, or software implementation. If such services are required, we will refer you to an appropriately qualified specialist or provide a separate engagement.

Assumptions & reliance: Our advice relies on information you provide and is not independently verified. Outcomes depend on timely implementation and may differ due to external factors. All modelling uses rule settings current at the report date and may change with law updates.

Key principle: Clarity is protection. When scope, exclusions, roles, and change control are explicit, you reduce risk, prevent write-offs, and maintain a professional, profitable, and trusted advisory relationship.

Engagement letters and documentation

In advisory, nothing protects you more than clarity. An engagement letter is not just a formality — it's your insurance policy. It sets the ground rules, manages risk, and positions you as the professional in control of the process. Without it, you're exposed. With it, you have certainty, structure, and confidence.

Why engagement letters matter

When you're delivering Top 20% benchmarking and advisory services, you're moving beyond compliance. That means you're also moving into higher expectations, more judgment calls, and potentially greater risk. A well-structured engagement letter locks down:

- Scope — what's in, and just as important, what's out.
- Responsibilities — the client must supply complete and accurate data; you deliver the analysis and advice.
- Expectations — fees, timing, deliverables, meetings, and reporting cycles.
- Compliance — you're covered under accounting and ethical standards.
- Protection — in the event of a dispute, you have the signed record on your side.

If you don't set the rules in writing, you invite trouble.

The non-negotiables to include

Every engagement letter for benchmarking and advisory should cover the essentials. At a minimum, include:

- Services — spell out what you are providing (benchmarking reports, advisory meetings, strategy recommendations, follow-ups).
- Boundaries — no audit, no legal or financial product advice, no assurance services. Make it crystal clear.
- Fees — how you charge (fixed, value-based, package), when you bill, and what happens if clients don't pay.
- Client responsibilities — they own the data, they must give you accurate records, and they're responsible for implementation.
- Confidentiality — confirm their information is protected.

- Disclaimers — benchmarking is advice, not a guarantee. Future performance is in their hands.
- Termination clause — covers how either party can exit the agreement.

Documentation beyond the letter

The engagement letter sets the framework, but documentation is an ongoing discipline. Build a file that can withstand scrutiny. That means:

- Advisory meeting notes — who was there, what was discussed, decisions made, agreed action steps.
- Strategy records — which strategies you presented, which the client chose, and why.
- Progress notes — emails, check-ins, reminders — document the trail.
- Risk notes — if the client rejects your advice or takes a different path, write it down and confirm it back to them.

Best practice

- Use templates — don't reinvent the wheel each time.
- Review and update engagement letters annually or when the scope changes.
- Keep everything securely stored and easy to access.
- Apply the golden rule: If it's not documented, it didn't happen.

Management client expectations

Managing expectations is where advisory success is either built or broken. Clients don't judge you on how clever your analysis is — they judge you on whether you deliver what they thought they were getting. If expectations are misaligned, even great results can turn into frustration. Get it right from the start, and you protect yourself, build trust, and foster a long-term relationship.

Be clear up front

Advisory is not compliance. There are no black-and-white rules, no single "right" answer, and no guaranteed outcomes. Clients need to hear this clearly. At the start of every engagement, spell out:

- What you will deliver — reports, benchmarking insights, strategy recommendations, and meetings.
- What you won't deliver — legal advice, investment recommendations, or guarantees.
- The client's role — their results depend on their own decisions and implementation, not just your advice.

The more explicit you are up front, the less risk you face down the track.

Under-promise, over-deliver

Never promise what you can't control. Benchmarks highlight gaps, and strategies point to improvements — but many variables influence business performance. Position yourself as the expert guide, not the miracle worker. Instead of "We'll double your profit," say "We'll show you where you can close the gap on the top 20% and provide practical strategies to move towards that level."

Clients will respect honesty. And when you exceed expectations, they'll value you more.

Set boundaries and stick to them.

Advisory work can quickly expand if you don't set boundaries. Clients will push — "can you also do this…?" — and scope creep is the fastest way to lose profitability and increase risk. Your job is to:

- Tie back every service to the engagement letter.
- Politely but firmly redirect when requests fall outside scope.

- Offer additional services with transparent pricing when appropriate.

Boundaries show you're a professional, not just a "yes person."

Ongoing communication

Managing expectations isn't a one-off — it's ongoing. That means:
- Reconfirming the process at key stages.
- Checking in to ensure clients understand what the numbers mean.
- Updating clients when timelines or deliverables shift.
- Documenting conversations so there's no room for doubt.

The key principle

Unmet expectations create risk. Clear expectations create loyalty. The difference comes down to how disciplined you are in managing the client relationship.

Protecting the accountant

In advisory work, protecting the client is always at the forefront of mind — but protecting the accountant is equally critical. Advisory engagements carry higher expectations, greater reliance on professional judgement, and more potential for disputes than standard compliance work. If you don't proactively safeguard yourself, you risk exposure to complaints, reputational damage, and even legal action.

1. Document everything

Every piece of advice, every recommendation, and every client decision must be appropriately documented. Advisory isn't about casual conversations — it's about providing a professional service with long-term consequences. File notes, signed reports, meeting summaries, and emails that confirm the client's understanding all form your first line of defence if things go wrong. The principle is simple: if it's not documented, it didn't happen.

2. Stay within your scope
Advisory requires clear boundaries. Protect yourself by defining precisely what you are (and are not) advising on. When benchmarking a business, you compare KPIs, provide insights, and recommend strategies. You are not giving legal opinions, financial product advice, or guarantees of outcomes. Clearly state these limitations in engagement letters and reinforce them in discussions.

3. Rely on quality control systems
Protecting the accountant means building safeguards into your practice. This includes:
- Peer review: Have another practitioner check high-risk advice.
- Software support: Use systems like TaxFitness to ensure benchmarking data, strategies, and reports are consistent and reliable.
- Checklists and templates: Standardised processes reduce human error and demonstrate professionalism.

4. Manage client expectations
Disputes usually arise from mismatched expectations. Clients may think advisory guarantees results — it doesn't. Protect yourself by being upfront: you provide expert insights and strategies, but implementation and results are the client's responsibility. Clear communication about the advisory journey (including risks, timelines, and variables outside your control) protects both you and the client.

5. Professional indemnity insurance

Finally, advisory services should always be underpinned by robust professional indemnity insurance. Confirm with your insurer that your policy covers advisory, benchmarking, and strategic consulting — not just tax compliance. Don't assume; check the fine print. A claim may never arise, but the protection must always be in place.

Key principle: Protecting the accountant is not about being defensive — it's about being professional. When you operate with clear boundaries, strong documentation, and robust systems, you can deliver high-value advisory services confidently, without fear of exposure.

Balancing opportunity and risk

The power of benchmarking lies in comparing a client's numbers against the Top 20% of businesses in their industry. This immediately reveals two sides of the equation: **opportunity** (where the client has room to improve) and risk (where they may be exposed or underperforming). The accountant's role is to help the client understand both and guide them towards improvements that lift performance while managing risk.

1. Opportunity through benchmarking

Benchmarking highlights where profit levers can be pulled. For example:
- Wages may be 8% above the Top 20% benchmark — an opportunity to improve efficiency.
- Rent might be 4% higher — an opportunity to renegotiate or relocate.
- Gross profit margin may lag by 10% — an opportunity to refine pricing or reduce discounts.

Each gap represents a measurable path to higher profitability. By quantifying these, the accountant demonstrates to clients what's possible if they perform at the best level in their industry.

2. Risk exposed by benchmarking

At the same time, benchmarking shines a light on risks that could damage the business if left unchecked:

- Excessive subcontractor use compared to the Top 20% exposes reliance on external labour.
- Below-benchmark owner's compensation may indicate cash flow pressure or underpricing.
- High overheads compared to the Top 20% suggest the business may struggle to weather downturns.

Ignoring these risks leaves the client vulnerable, even if revenues are growing.

3. Balancing the two in advisory

The best advisory conversations don't just celebrate opportunities or dwell on risks — they strike a balance between both. For example:

- Cutting wages too aggressively may create short-term profit but damage service quality.
- Expanding sales to close a revenue gap may require upfront marketing investment, with uncertain results.
- Reducing rent by relocating may lower costs but also disrupt operations.

Advisors must present both the benefit and the trade-off, ensuring clients make informed decisions.

4. Building credibility through balance

Accountants protect themselves and serve clients best when they are seen as balanced advisors — not cheerleaders for opportunity, and not fearmongers about risk. The Top 20% benchmarks provide the objective yardstick: they are not opinion, but data. By positioning recommendations against industry best performers, accountants keep conversations grounded in fact rather than guesswork.

Key principle: Top 20% benchmarking is effective because it addresses reality. The data shows where the opportunities lie — and where risks are already embedded in the numbers. The accountant's role is to strike the right balance, helping clients move towards Top 20% performance without overreaching or exposing themselves unnecessarily.

Case studies – Risk managed well vs poorly

Numbers tell a story, but how an accountant interprets and acts on them makes the difference between success and failure. The following case studies illustrate how benchmarking can highlight both opportunities and risks — and how managing that risk effectively (or ineffectively) directly impacts the outcome.

Case study 1 – Café: wage costs

Benchmark insight: The café's wages were 42% of sales, compared to the Top 20% benchmark of 35%.

- Risk managed well: The accountant explained that simply cutting staff would damage service quality. Instead, they recommended adjusting rostering, cross-training staff, and increasing menu prices by 5% to improve gross margin. Within 12 months, wage costs dropped to 37% without hurting customer experience.

- Risk managed poorly: Another café owner, desperate to hit the benchmark, cut staff aggressively to bring wages down to 33%. Service slowed, customer complaints increased, and within six months, sales declined by 15%. Chasing the benchmark without managing the associated risk led to long-term damage.

Case study 2 – Plumbing business: subcontractor reliance

Benchmark insight: Subcontractor costs accounted for 28% of sales, compared to the Top 20% benchmark of 15%.

- Risk managed well: The accountant highlighted the risk of over-reliance on subcontractors, which includes higher costs and less control. Together, they developed a plan to hire two full-time tradespeople and renegotiate the rates of subcontractors. Within 18 months, subcontractor costs dropped to 18% and margins improved.
- Risk managed poorly: Another plumber ignored the risk, arguing that subcontractors gave "flexibility." When demand slowed, subcontractors continued to absorb the majority of jobs, leaving business owners with low profit margins. The business failed to build equity in staff and systems.

Key principles of risk management in advisory

Advisory work presents numerous opportunities for accountants to enhance their client relationships and increase practice revenue. However, it also introduces a range of risks that must be actively managed. The key is to strike the right balance between seizing opportunity and protecting both the client and the accountant. The following principles underpin effective risk management in the Top 20% of business advisory firms.

1. Clarity of scope and boundaries

Every advisory engagement should start with a clearly defined scope. Accountants must specify what is included—and equally important, what is excluded. This reduces misunderstandings, ensures that expectations are realistic, and provides a clear reference point in case disputes arise. Clearly documented engagement letters are the foundation.

2. Evidence-based advice

Data, not opinion, should support recommendations. Benchmarking against the top 20% of businesses in an industry provides a strong evidence base. This reinforces credibility, minimises exposure to claims of negligence, and demonstrates a professional, objective process rather than a subjective judgment.

3. Professional and ethical standards

Risk management encompasses not only legal protection but also ethics and reputation. Accountants must act in the client's best interests, avoid conflicts of interest, and disclose limitations. Maintaining professional objectivity and integrity protects the practice's long-term brand.

4. Compliance with legal obligations

Advisory services must always remain within the boundaries of the law and relevant regulatory frameworks. Accountants must understand what falls under licensed activities (such as financial product advice) and what does not—staying compliant safeguards both the practice and the client.

5. Documentation and record-keeping

If it isn't documented, it didn't happen. Comprehensive notes of meetings, data sources, and reasoning behind recommendations are essential. Documentation not only provides legal protection but also demonstrates professionalism to clients.

6. Client education and transparency

Advisory outcomes depend on client decisions and the implementation of those decisions. Clients must understand that benchmarking highlights opportunities and risks, but the responsibility for acting on strategies is shared. Transparent communication ensures clients are aware of limitations and potential risks.

7. Insurance and liability protection

Professional indemnity insurance should always cover advisory services, not just compliance. Accountants must ensure their policies extend to business advisory activities, including benchmarking and strategic recommendations. Risk management involves both transferring and reducing risk.

8. Continuous review and quality control

Advisory risk management is ongoing. Systems, processes, and reports must be regularly reviewed to ensure accuracy and consistency. Periodic internal checks, peer reviews, and regression testing of software outputs reduce the risk of errors slipping through.

9. Balance between innovation and caution

The top 20% of business advisory services require innovation—identifying gaps, suggesting new strategies, and guiding clients toward improved performance. At the same time, accountants must apply professional caution. Every recommendation should strike a balance between potential upside and consideration of the risks.

16.

Avoiding the common benchmarking mistakes

'THE MOST DANGEROUS KIND OF WASTE IS THE WASTE WE DO NOT RECOGNISE'

– SHIGEO SHINGO (JAPANESE INDUSTRIAL ENGINEER AND A WORLD-LEADING EXPERT IN MANUFACTURING EFFICIENCY AND QUALITY MANAGEMENT. WIDELY ACKNOWLEDGED FOR HIS WORK IN FORMALISING AND TEACHING THE PRINCIPLES BEHIND THE TOYOTA PRODUCTION SYSTEM (1960S).

Introduction

Benchmarking is one of the most powerful tools available to accountants. Done well, it provides clarity, reveals hidden opportunities, and drives clients toward Top 20% performance. Done poorly, it undermines trust, confuses clients, and risks damaging your credibility as an advisor.

The reality is simple: benchmarking mistakes are common. They happen because accountants are busy, client data isn't always clean, and shortcuts can be tempting. But every mistake reduces the value of your benchmarking service — and in advisory, perception and trust are everything.

This chapter highlights the most frequent mistakes, why they occur, the risks they create, and the simple steps you can take to avoid them. By recognising and correcting these pitfalls, you'll ensure your benchmarking advice is accurate, persuasive, and consistently positioned at the Top 20% standard.

Focusing on averages instead of Top 20%

Why it happens: Averages are easy. They're simple to calculate, widely available, and often used in generic industry surveys.

Why it's dangerous: Averages blend high and low performers into mediocrity. A client who is "better than average" may still be far behind the industry leaders, while one just below average may actually be a low performer if measured against the Top 20%. Averages provide comfort, not insight.

What to do instead: Always benchmark against the Top 20%. These businesses show what is possible. They provide a performance standard worth pursuing and give clients a roadmap to join the leaders in their industry.

Case study: A suburban café compared its wage costs to the industry average and was satisfied it was "better than most." Yet, when compared to the Top 20% benchmark, wages were 8% higher than the leaders. The owner thought they were efficient, but they were leaving $70,000 in annual profit on the table. By shifting the comparison to the Top 20%, the accountant reframed the conversation and drove rostering improvements that closed the gap within a year.

Using inaccurate or incomplete data

Why it happens: Clients often provide financials that are outdated, misclassified, or inconsistent. Accountants under pressure may accept the data at face value.

Why it's dangerous: Bad data equals bad advice. If costs are misclassified, KPIs will be distorted. If revenue is missing, margins will look artificially weak. The client may then make poor decisions based on flawed analysis.

What to do instead: Build discipline into your process. Validate client data before benchmarking. Reconcile figures, check classifications, and ask probing questions. Ensure your comparisons are based on accurate and complete numbers.

Case study: A plumbing business submitted management accounts where subcontractor costs were misclassified as wages. Benchmarking against this distorted data suggested they were overspending on salaries compared to the Top 20%. The client panicked and considered cutting staff. Once the error was corrected, it became clear that their labour model was sound — the real issue was the overuse of subcontractors. A mistake avoided, and a far better strategy identified.

Ignoring industry context and client circumstances

Why it happens: Accountants sometimes present benchmarks in isolation, without considering the unique factors that shape the client's business — such as location, business model, or size.

Why it's dangerous: Benchmarks without context can mislead. For example, a café in a regional town won't have the same rent profile as one in a CBD high-rise. Ignoring these differences makes clients feel benchmarking is irrelevant or unfair.

What to do instead: Interpret benchmarks through the client's reality. Highlight the numbers but explain the "why" behind them. Use the benchmarks to spark a conversation, not dictate a judgment.

Case study: A regional butcher compared their rent to national benchmarks and appeared to be overpaying for it. The accountant initially flagged rent as a critical issue. However, after considering the context — a prime central street location with higher foot traffic — it was clear that the rent was justified. In fact, relocating would have destroyed sales. The benchmark was accurate, but without context, it nearly led to the wrong advice.

Overloading reports with too many KPI's

Why it happens: Accountants aim to demonstrate thoroughness and value by including every available KPI in the report.

Why it's dangerous: Too much data overwhelms clients. They don't know where to focus, and the most critical insights get lost in the noise. Overloaded reports reduce clarity instead of increasing it.

What to do instead: Focus on the critical few. Highlight the 5–7 KPIs that matter most for the client's business model and strategy. Position the rest as supporting information, not the main story.

Case study: A small bookkeeping firm presented a benchmarking report with 28 KPIs. The client felt overwhelmed, admitted they "couldn't make sense of it all," and disengaged from the process. At the subsequent review, the accountant focused on five key KPIs: wages, overhead, net profit margin, client retention, and owners' compensation. Suddenly, the conversation shifted from confusion to clarity — and the client signed up for quarterly advisory meetings.

Failing to translate numbers into strategies

Why it happens: Some accountants stop at presenting the numbers. They highlight the gap to Top 20% benchmarks, but fail to translate this into practical steps the client can take.

Why it's dangerous: Numbers without strategies frustrate clients.

They know what the problem is, but leave the meeting unsure how to fix it. The accountant appears to be a statistician, rather than an advisor.

What to do instead: Always bridge the gap. For every key benchmark variance, recommend a strategy. If wages are too high, suggest rostering reviews or process automation. If rent is excessive, consider exploring relocation or renegotiation options to find a more affordable solution. Move from insights to actions.

Case study: A retail clothing store received a benchmarking report that highlighted its rent was 5% above the Top 20%. The accountant stopped there. The owner left the meeting frustrated, knowing "the problem" but not what to do. A year later, after working with a different accountant, the same client received specific strategies — renegotiating the lease and subleasing unused space. That accountant delivered results and won a loyal client for life.

Presenting results without a narrative

Why it happens: Accountants sometimes hand over benchmarking reports as if the data speaks for itself.

Why it's dangerous: Clients don't interpret data the way accountants do. Without a story, the numbers are confusing, even intimidating. This erodes engagement and reduces the likelihood of follow-through.

What to do instead: Position the report as a conversation tool. Walk the client through the flow: here's where you are, here's where the Top 20% are, here's the gap, and here's how to close it. Anchor every number in a narrative that makes sense to the client.

Case study: A dental practice received a detailed benchmarking report but no explanation. The owner flicked through the charts, found it "too technical," and filed it away. Nothing changed. Later, the same report was presented by another advisor, who walked through a straightforward narrative: "Here's your performance today, here's what the top practices achieve, here's the gap, and here's how to close it." That straightforward narrative transformed the client's engagement and opened the door to $50,000 in new advisory fees.

Benchmarking once, instead of regularly

Why it happens: Many accountants see benchmarking as a "one-off" exercise, done to impress a client or tick a box.

Why it's dangerous: A single benchmarking report is a snapshot. It quickly becomes outdated. Without follow-up, progress is invisible and accountability fades. Clients don't see improvement, so they don't see value.

What to do instead: Make benchmarking a regular service. Conduct reviews annually, or better still, quarterly. Show progress over time, reinforce accountability, and lock in long-term advisory engagements.

Case study: A trades business received a one-off benchmarking report in 2021. The insights were valuable, but no follow-up was conducted. Two years later, the client said, "That was interesting, but nothing really happened." Another firm began quarterly benchmarking with the same client, tracking progress KPI by KPI. The client could see improvements every three months and continued to pay for the ongoing service. Benchmarking once is a transaction. Benchmarking regularly is a relationship.

Overpromising outcomes from benchmarking

Why it happens: In the enthusiasm to win work, some accountants suggest that benchmarking will instantly transform profitability.

Why it's dangerous: Benchmarking is powerful, but it is not a magic bullet. Over-promising creates unrealistic expectations. When improvements take longer, the client becomes disappointed and may lose trust in the project.

What to do instead: Position benchmarking honestly. It highlights opportunities, guides strategy, and drives improvement — but results require consistent effort. Under-promise and over-deliver. That is how trust is built.

Case study: An accountant told a fitness studio owner that benchmarking would "double profits in six months." When results took longer, the client lost faith and cancelled the service. By contrast, another advisor with a different client positioned benchmarking as a tool to "identify opportunities and build long-term strategies." Improvements came steadily, expectations were managed, and the client saw the accountant as a trusted partner — not a salesman who over-promised.

Conclusion

Benchmarking is only as powerful as the process behind it. When accountants fall into the trap of relying on averages, accepting flawed data, ignoring context, or simply presenting numbers without a narrative, the value of benchmarking is compromised. Worse, these mistakes can damage client trust and undermine your position as an advisor.

But every mistake is avoidable. By benchmarking against the Top 20%, validating client data, focusing on the critical few

KPIs, providing context, and linking every insight to a strategy, you transform benchmarking into one of the most compelling advisory tools in your practice. By incorporating a straightforward narrative and a commitment to regular reviews, you create a service that drives accountability, delivers results, and fosters long-term client relationships.

The difference between average accountants and top-performing advisors is not just the data they use, but the discipline and professionalism with which they apply it. Avoid these common mistakes, and you'll not only protect yourself — you'll inspire clients with a vision of what's possible when they aim for the Top 20%.

17

The future of Top 20% business benchmarking & advisory

'GOOD IS THE ENEMY OF GREAT'

– JIM COLLINS (GLOBALLY RECOGNISED BUSINESS
RESEARCHER AND AUTHOR, BEST KNOWN FOR HIS
BESTSELLING BOOK GOOD TO GREAT. HIS WORK FOCUSES ON
WHY SOME COMPANIES OUTPERFORM OTHERS AND WHAT
MAKES GREAT BUSINESSES ENDURE OVER TIME (2001).

Introduction

Business benchmarking and advisory are moving faster than ever. What used to be a slow, manual, number-crunching job has become a strategic process powered by technology, data, and AI. Clients don't want reports anymore — they want insight, context, and a roadmap to Top 20% performance. For accountants, that's both the opportunity and the responsibility. The future belongs to firms that can combine benchmarking data with sharp advisory skills to deliver measurable business outcomes.

The next decade isn't about who has the best numbers. It's about who can interpret those numbers, integrate them seamlessly with technology, and deliver advice at scale without losing personal impact. AI, cloud platforms, real-time data feeds, and predictive analytics are revolutionising the way accountants gather information, identify opportunities, and engage in conversations with clients.

But this isn't just about tech. Clients are expecting more, faster, and with more profound relevance. Ethical and professional standards must evolve in the digital age to make sure insights are delivered with integrity. And accountants can't just think local anymore — benchmarking is now a global language of performance. The businesses you serve are already being compared against international standards, whether you're ready or not.

This chapter sets out the future of benchmarking and advisory through eight lenses that will define where the profession goes next:

1. **Technology driving change** – AI and automation aren't optional; they're reshaping how you work.
2. **Real-time benchmarking becomes the standard** – instant comparisons will transform client conversations.
3. **Advisory at scale without losing personalisation** – the firms that win will master efficiency without becoming generic.
4. **Rising client expectations** – business owners want more insight, more often, with less fluff.
5. **Professional and ethical standards in the digital age** – the guardrails accountants must keep as data drives decisions.
6. **Global perspective** – Benchmarking across industries and economies – benchmarking is a worldwide movement, and accountants must align with it.
7. **Opportunities for accountants who lead** – the firms that step up first will dominate the market.
8. **Conclusion** – advisory and benchmarking aren't optional anymore. They are the profession's future.

For accountants who embrace these changes, the future isn't a threat. It's the most significant chance in a generation to lock in your role as the trusted advisor every business owner needs.

Technology driving change

The most significant driver shaping the future of benchmarking and advisory is technology. What once took hours of manual number-crunching can now be automated in minutes. The accountant's role is shifting — away from gathering and formatting data, and toward interpreting it, applying judgment, and guiding clients.

AI-powered insights

Artificial intelligence is transforming benchmarking. Instead of simply identifying gaps, AI can recommend strategies tailored to the client's circumstances. It doesn't replace the accountant, but it accelerates the process and expands capacity. Where an accountant once had time to prepare benchmarking for 10 clients, AI now makes it possible to deliver the service to 50 — without sacrificing quality.

Predictive analytics

Traditional benchmarking is backward-looking. It tells us how the client performed compared to the Top 20% last year. The next evolution is predictive analytics — using data trends to forecast where performance is likely to head. This enables accountants to intervene earlier, allowing clients to make proactive decisions rather than reacting after the fact.

Automated data integration

Manual data entry and spreadsheet uploads are rapidly disappearing. Benchmarking platforms now integrate directly with accounting systems such as Xero, MYOB, and QuickBooks. This eliminates human error, saves time, and enables accountants to instantly refresh benchmarks. The result is more accurate insights and a smoother client experience.

Cloud platforms and connectivity

The rise of cloud technology means benchmarking is no longer tied to static reports. Dashboards can be accessed anytime, anywhere, and shared easily with clients during advisory meetings. Integration across apps — from accounting to CRM to cash flow forecasting — ensures benchmarking isn't an isolated tool, but part of a broader ecosystem that supports informed decision-making.

The takeaway is clear: technology is not replacing the accountant. It is removing the low-value work and magnifying the high-value role — interpretation, strategy, and client engagement. The firms that embrace this shift will lead the future of Top 20% business benchmarking and advisory.

Real-time benchmarking becomes the standard.

The days of benchmarking as a once-a-year exercise are numbered. Annual reports may highlight opportunities, but they are snapshots — quickly outdated and often forgotten. The future of benchmarking lies in real-time, continuous, and embedded processes within the advisory process.

From snapshots to live dashboards

Static reports provide an overview of events that occurred in the past year. Real-time dashboards display what is happening in real-time. Accountants can instantly compare a client's KPIs to the Top 20% and identify issues as they emerge, not months later. This shift moves benchmarking from a rear-view mirror to a live GPS for business performance.

Continuous KPI tracking

When data flows directly from the client's accounting system, benchmarking becomes dynamic. KPIs can be tracked on a monthly or even weekly basis. Instead of waiting for annual reviews, clients see progress — or slippage — in near real-time. This creates accountability and momentum.

From reactive advice to proactive intervention

Traditional benchmarking was reactive: "Here's where you fell short last year." Real-time benchmarking allows accountants to be proactive: "Your wages are drifting above Top 20% benchmarks this quarter — let's act now before it erodes profit." This transforms the accountant's role from commentator to coach, guiding clients in real time.

Client expectations are rising.

In a digital-first world, clients expect the same immediacy in advisory services that they receive from apps in their daily lives. They won't be satisfied waiting twelve months to learn their rent is too high or their net profit margin is lagging. Real-time benchmarking will soon be the standard that clients demand.

The message is simple: in the future, benchmarking will no longer be an event — it will be a process. Firms that adopt real-time benchmarking will deepen engagement, strengthen client loyalty, and position themselves as indispensable advisors.

Advisory at scale without losing personalisation

One of the most significant challenges for accounting firms is balancing scale with personalisation. Benchmarking and advisory services are high-value offerings, but they have traditionally been resource-intensive — meaning only a handful of clients could receive them. The future changes this equation.

Scaling advisory with technology

AI-driven platforms, automated data feeds, and templated processes enable accountants to deliver benchmarking and advisory services to dozens, even hundreds, of clients with significantly less manual effort. What once took days can be completed in minutes. This scalability enables firms to expand advisory revenue without incurring the same level of staff costs.

Standardising the process

The danger of scale is inconsistency. Without structure, advisory becomes hit-and-miss. That's why systems like the TaxFitness 10-Step Top 20% Business Benchmarking Process are critical. They give every advisor in the firm a repeatable framework — ensuring the same high-quality service is delivered, whether to the first client or the hundredth.

Keeping It personal

Clients don't want generic advice. They want insights tailored to their business, delivered in plain language, and connected to their goals. Technology enables efficiency, but it is the accountant's interpretation, judgment, and relationship-building that create value. The key is to utilise automation for the heavy lifting, then reinvest the saved time into more high-quality conversations with clients.

The competitive advantage

Firms that master advisory at scale without losing personalisation will dominate the market. They'll serve more clients, create deeper relationships, and build recurring revenue streams. Those who fail to scale will be left behind, delivering benchmarking as a one-off report while competitors deliver it as an ongoing, value-driven service.

The future belongs to firms that can deliver high-quality, personalised advisory — not just to a select few clients, but across their entire client base.

Rising client expectations

Client expectations are shifting rapidly. Compliance work alone is no longer enough to hold a client relationship. Business owners want more insight, more context, and more guidance — and they expect their accountant to deliver it. Benchmarking and advisory are at the centre of this demand.

Beyond numbers to insights

Clients don't just want to know where they sit against benchmarks — they want to understand why. They expect their accountant to interpret the numbers, explain the drivers, and outline practical steps. A benchmarking report without explanation feels like a dead end. What clients really value is the conversation it sparks.

Demand for ongoing advisory

A once-a-year benchmarking review no longer meets the mark. Business owners expect their accountant to be a partner in improvement — tracking progress, flagging issues early, and helping them adjust strategies along the way. The best accountants are positioning benchmarking as part of a regular advisory service, not a stand-alone exercise.

The accountant as business coach

Clients are increasingly seeing their accountant not just as a tax expert, but also as a business coach. They expect guidance on strategy, cash flow, staffing, pricing, and risk. Benchmarking is the perfect platform for this shift because it grounds the discussion in data and positions the accountant as a forward-looking advisor.

Rising standards of delivery

Technology and competition are raising the bar. Clients compare their accountant's services to the apps they use every day — seamless, fast, and easy to understand. Long, technical reports and jargon-heavy presentations are no longer acceptable. The firms that thrive will be those that make benchmarking simple, clear, and directly connected to the client's goals.

The takeaway is clear: clients want more than data. They want meaning, direction, and accountability. Accountants who deliver this will deepen trust, lock in loyalty, and stand apart from firms that still treat benchmarking as just a set of numbers.

Professional and ethical standards in the digital age

As technology reshapes benchmarking and advisory, the accountant's professional and ethical obligations remain unchanged — but the way they must be applied is evolving. The future will not only demand stronger technical skills but also a heightened sense of responsibility in managing data, AI, and advice.

Avoiding over-reliance on AI

AI can analyse data and suggest strategies at speed, but it cannot replace human judgment. The risk is that accountants present AI outputs as fact without applying professional scepticism. If recommendations are followed blindly, the client may take actions that are unsuitable or even harmful. The role of the accountant is to filter AI insights through professional expertise, ensuring advice is both accurate and appropriate.

Data privacy and security

With benchmarking increasingly cloud-based and integrated with multiple systems, protecting client data is paramount.

Cybersecurity is no longer just an IT issue — it is an ethical obligation. Accountants must ensure that platforms are secure, access is controlled, and client confidentiality is never compromised.

Maintaining independence and integrity

Digital tools may introduce conflicts of interest — for example, software platforms recommending add-on products or services. Accountants must remain clear: their duty is to the client, not to the technology provider. Independence and integrity must be safeguarded, even as new business models emerge.

Future regulatory pressures

As AI and automation reshape the advisory landscape, regulators will step in. Standards will evolve to govern how benchmarking is delivered, how AI-generated outputs are utilised, and how data is managed. Accountants who build ethical discipline into their processes now will be well-placed to adapt as compliance expectations tighten.

The principle is simple: technology may change, but professional standards do not. The future accountant will combine the power of digital tools with the timeless values of accuracy, scepticism, confidentiality, and integrity. That is how trust is maintained in an era of rapid change.

Global perspective – Benchmarking across industries and economies

Benchmarking isn't just an Australian idea. It's a global discipline that shapes industries, drives competition, and sets new standards for performance across every economy. If accountants want to stay relevant, they need to see benchmarking not just as a local tool, but as part of a worldwide movement.

Different industries, same principle

Whether it's retail in New York, manufacturing in Germany, or technology in Singapore, the principle is the same: the top performers define the benchmark, and everyone else measures against it. Global competition means businesses can no longer hide behind borders. A café in Perth is effectively competing with chains refining their models in London or Tokyo.

Economies that embrace benchmarking move faster

Countries and industries that institutionalise benchmarking — using data to improve efficiency, profitability, and client outcomes — consistently outpace those that don't. This is why multinationals and world-class organisations are relentless in their pursuit of metrics. They measure everything, compare constantly, and continually strive for improvement. Small business owners expect the same level of support from their accountants.

The global opportunity for accountants

This creates an enormous opportunity for accountants who lead. By positioning benchmarking within their advisory services, they aren't just competing with the firm down the road — they're aligning their clients with world-class standards. That's powerful. Business owners want to know: "How do I stack up, not just against my neighbour, but against the best in the world?" Accountants who can answer that question are untouchable in their market.

Benchmarking as the universal advisory language

Tax law is local. Compliance is local. But benchmarking is universal. The same KPIs — profit margin, wages, rent, subcontractors, overheads — apply everywhere. That's why benchmarking is emerging as the common language of business advisory globally.

What this means for you

The future is clear. Accountants who ignore benchmarking will be sidelined by consultants, advisors, and technology platforms that operate on a global scale. Those who embrace it will lead, because they'll offer clients more than just compliance — they'll provide perspective. Local numbers are viewed against international standards. Advice that stands up anywhere.

"Benchmarking is the search for industry best practices that lead to superior performance."
– Robert C. Camp, Father of Benchmarking.

Opportunities for accountants who lead

The shift to technology-enabled benchmarking and advisory is not a threat — it is the single most significant opportunity accountants have seen in decades. Firms that lead the way will cultivate deeper client relationships, generate recurring revenue, and establish themselves as essential partners in driving business success.

Differentiate in a crowded market.

Most accountants still compete on compliance. By embedding Top 20% benchmarking and advisory into your service model, you immediately stand out. You're no longer "just another accountant" — you're the advisor who helps clients move from average performance to elite performance.

Deepen client relationships

Benchmarking is not abstract. It touches on wages, rent, margins, and owners' profit — the levers that really matter to business owners. Discussing these issues regularly builds trust at a strategic level. Clients stop seeing you as a cost and start seeing you as an investment.

Expand advisory revenue

Each benchmarking conversation naturally leads to projects, including cost reviews, pricing strategies, process improvements, and risk management. Advisory revenue is no longer separate from compliance; it flows directly from it. Firms that systemise this process can add tens or even hundreds of thousands of dollars in new fees each year.

Build firm value

Recurring advisory income, supported by structured processes and technology, builds firm value. Buyers pay higher multiples for practices that can demonstrate sustainable, scalable revenue beyond tax returns. Benchmarking isn't just suitable for clients — it directly increases the accountant's own business value.

Shape the future of the profession.

Accountants who adopt Top 20% benchmarking and advisory services early will help shape the evolution of the profession. They will set the standards, capture the best clients, and attract the most talented staff. They will move from compliance reporters to strategic advisors — a role that cannot be automated away.

The opportunity is clear: firms that embrace the future will not just survive — they will lead.

Conclusions

The future of benchmarking and advisory is already here. Technology, AI, and real-time data are transforming what accountants can deliver — but the fundamentals remain the same. Clients want clarity, context, and direction. They want to know how they compare to the best, and what they must do to close the gap.

For accountants, the choice is simple: evolve or be left behind.

Those who rely solely on compliance-only services will see their relevance diminish. Those who embrace Top 20% benchmarking, leverage technology, and combine it with professional judgment will secure their place at the centre of their clients' success.

The opportunity has never been greater. By avoiding the mistakes of the past, adopting the tools of the future, and adhering to ethical and professional standards, accountants can redefine their role — not as mere reporters of history, but as architects of business performance.

The firms that lead this shift will capture more clients, grow stronger relationships, and build enduring value. The future of Top 20% benchmarking and advisory isn't just about data — it's about shaping businesses, transforming practices, and elevating the profession itself.

18.

Case studies – Benchmarking in action

"IN A WORLD OF ACCELERATING CHANGE, THE WINNERS WILL BE THOSE WHO MEASURE BETTER, LEARN FASTER, AND ACT WITH MORE DISCIPLINE."

– JIM COLLINS.

Case study 1: café – Turning around a hospitality business

The business

A suburban café with 12 staff and an annual turnover of $1.8 million. Strong community presence and good foot traffic, but struggling to make consistent profits.

The benchmark gap

Compared against the Top 20% benchmarks for cafés:

- Wages were at 48% of turnover (benchmark: 32–36%)
- COGS were at 38% (benchmark: 28–32%)
- Rent was 14% of turnover (benchmark: under 10%)
- Net profit was 2% (benchmark: 12%+)

The café was working hard but sitting in the bottom 40% of performance.

Strategies applied

1. **Roster discipline** – Benchmarking exposed excessive weekend and penalty-hour wages. The owner introduced

split shifts and monitored wage % daily.

2. **Menu engineering** – Identified low-margin items dragging down COGS. Re-priced coffee sizes, removed two unprofitable food lines, and focused on high-margin add-ons.

3. **Supplier renegotiation** – Benchmarks highlighted above-market costs for milk and baked goods. Switched suppliers and secured volume discounts.

4. **Lease restructure** – The Accountant used benchmarking data to justify a rent review. Achieved a rent reduction over three years, bringing occupancy closer to the benchmark.

The results
Within 12 months:
- Wages reduced to 36% of turnover
- COGS dropped to 31%
- Rent reduced to 11% of turnover
- Net profit lifted from 2% to 10%

The café moved from the bottom 40% to shy of the Top 20% performance. The owner now uses benchmarking reports on a quarterly basis, not only to monitor costs but also to motivate staff by showing progress against industry leaders.

Takeaway for accountants
This case shows the power of benchmarking to turn vague problems ("we're not making enough money") into measurable insights and actionable strategies. The accountant became more than a tax agent — they became the café's business coach and trusted advisor.

Case study 2: Electrical contracting business – Reducing subcontractor blowouts

The business

A family-owned electrical contracting business with eight employees and an annual turnover of $2.6 million. Work is split between residential projects and small commercial contracts. Despite strong demand, cash flow was tight and profits inconsistent.

The benchmark gap

Benchmarking against the Top 20% of trade businesses revealed:

- **Subcontractor costs** at 28% of turnover (benchmark: under 15%)
- **Gross margin** at 32% (benchmark: 45%+)
- **Overheads** at 22% (benchmark: 15–18%)
- **Net profit** at 5% (benchmark: 15%+)

The business was winning plenty of work but leaving too much money on the table.

Strategies applied

1. **Job costing discipline** – Introduced benchmarking-based job costing templates to capture proper margins per project. Quickly identified under-quoted jobs.
2. **Reduce subcontractor reliance** – Hired two full-time tradespeople to replace casual subcontractors. The wage percentage increased slightly, but subcontractor costs dropped dramatically.
3. **Supplier negotiation** – Used benchmark data to push back on key suppliers and secured bulk discounts and standardised materials list across projects.
4. **Overhead trim** – Benchmarks showed overheads 6–7%

higher than top performers. Implemented cloud job management software, cut admin duplication, and renegotiated vehicle leases.

The results

Within 9 months:

- Subcontractor costs reduced from 28% to 16% of turnover
- Gross margin improved from 32% to 44%
- Overheads reduced from 22% to 18%
- Net profit lifted from 5% to 13% — approaching Top 20% levels

Cash flow stabilised, the business built internal capacity, and the owners gained confidence to quote more aggressively, knowing they were benchmarking against the best.

Takeaway for accountants

Benchmarking reframed the client's thinking. Instead of just "we're busy but broke," the accountant showed exactly where the leaks were and how to plug them. By shifting reliance from subcontractors to employees, tightening job costing, and attacking overheads, the accountant turned compliance into real advisory value.

Case study 3: Independent retail store – Fixing stock turnover and rent pressures

The business

A family-owned homewares store in a suburban shopping strip—annual turnover of $1.4 million with six staff. Strong local reputation, but profits were razor-thin and cash flow was constantly under pressure.

The benchmark gap

Against the Top 20% benchmarks for retail:

- **Stock turnover** was 2.1 times a year (benchmark: 4–6 times)
- **Gross margin** sat at 39% (benchmark: 50%+)
- **Rent** was 16% of turnover (benchmark: under 10%)
- **Net profit** was 1% (benchmark: 8–12%)

The business was tying up too much cash in slow-moving stock and paying above-benchmark rent.

Strategies applied

1. **Inventory management** – Introduced a 90-day stock cycle target. Cleared out dead stock with clearance sales and tightened purchasing policies using benchmarks as the baseline.
2. **Supplier negotiations** – Benchmarks highlighted below-average gross margin. The accountant worked with the owner to renegotiate wholesale prices and introduce volume rebates.
3. **Margin focus** – Shifted product mix to higher-margin home décor lines and reduced reliance on low-margin bulk stock.
4. **Rent negotiation** – Used benchmarking data in lease discussions. The landlord agreed to a turnover rent model, reducing the fixed rent burden by 3%.

The results

Within 12 months:

- Stock turnover increased from 2.1x to 4.5x annually
- Gross margin lifted from 39% to 49%
- Rent reduced from 16% to 12% of turnover

- Net profit rose from 1% to 9% — firmly in Top 20% territory

The owner transitioned from "always broke despite sales" to achieving positive cash flow and a business that finally rewarded their efforts.

Takeaway for accountants
Retail benchmarks shine a light on the critical drivers — stock turnover, rent %, and margins. By tackling these complex data challenges, the accountant transformed a struggling store into a high-performing retail business. Benchmarking didn't just highlight the problems — it gave the owner confidence to act.

Case study 4: Small law firm – Lifting utilisation and profitability

The business
A boutique suburban law firm with three partners, seven staff, and a turnover of $2.2 million. The partners were working long hours, but profits were underwhelming compared to the effort.

The benchmark gap
Compared to the Top 20% of professional services firms:
- **Billable hours** utilisation was 62% (benchmark: 75%+)
- **Revenue per employee** was $190,000 (benchmark: $250,000+)
- **Overheads** were 32% of turnover (benchmark: 25%)
- **Net profit** was 12% (benchmark: 25%+)

The firm was carrying excess admin, pricing inconsistencies, and weak workflow management.

Strategies applied

1. **Time discipline** – Introduced daily timesheet reviews and accountability for fee earners. Lifted focus on billable vs non-billable hours.
2. **Pricing and packaging** – Benchmarks showed below-average revenue per employee. Shifted from hourly billing to fixed-fee packages for standard services, improving realisation rates.
3. **Delegation** – Partners were over-servicing low-value tasks. Benchmarks highlighted partner charge-out rates that were well above administrative work. Pushed more admin and paralegal work down.
4. **Overhead control** – Benchmarks exposed office rent and admin costs 6–7% above best performers. Downsized premises and streamlined admin team using cloud practice management.

The results

Within 12 months:

- Billable utilisation improved from 62% to 76%
- Revenue per employee increased from $190,000 to $245,000
- Overheads reduced from 32% to 26%
- Net profit margin rose from 12% to 23%

The firm doubled its bottom line without acquiring new clients, solely by benchmarking and aligning its performance with Top 20% standards.

Takeaway for accountants

Professional services firms often believe their problems are "unique." Benchmarking proves otherwise. The same drivers — utilisation, overheads, revenue per employee — are universal. By showing the gaps and coaching through changes, the accountant repositioned themselves as a strategic advisor, not just a compliance partner.

Case study 5: Family business group – Aligning multiple entities for Top 20% performance

The business

A second-generation family group operating three retail outlets, a small wholesale arm, and a property investment company—combined turnover of $6.5 million across four entities. The family wanted to grow, but constant disputes about cash flow, reinvestment, and succession were stalling decisions.

The benchmark gap

When benchmarked individually and as a group, the data revealed:

- **Retail outlets:** Gross margin at 42% (benchmark: 50%+), stock turnover 2.8x (benchmark: 4–6x).
- **Wholesale division:** Overheads at 28% (benchmark: under 20%).
- **Property company**: Return on equity at 3% (benchmark: 6–8%).
- **Group consolidated net profit:** 5% (benchmark: 12%+).

The family believed they were "doing fine," but benchmarking showed they were well below the Top 20%.

Strategies applied

1. **Entity-level transparency** – Benchmarks allowed each division to be measured separately. Family disputes shifted from opinion to fact.
2. **Retail improvement plan** – Cleared out old stock, tightened purchasing, and reset gross margin targets to match the Top 20%.

3. **Wholesale overhead restructure** – Moved warehousing to a shared facility, cutting overheads by 6%.
4. **Property company alignment** – Benchmarks exposed underperforming assets. Sold one low-yield property and reinvested in a higher-return commercial property.
5. **Succession and governance** – Used benchmarks to set clear performance targets for each entity and established quarterly family board meetings.

The results

Over 18 months:
- Retail gross margins improved from 42% to 49%, and stock turnover increased from 2.8x to 4.5x.
- Wholesale overheads dropped from 28% to 19%.
- Property ROE doubled from 3% to 6%.
- Consolidated group net profit rose from 5% to 11% — approaching Top 20% standards.
- Family conflict eased significantly, as discussions centred on agreed benchmark targets instead of personal opinions.

Takeaway for accountants

Benchmarking isn't just for single-entity SMEs. It's a powerful tool for family groups, especially where emotions and legacy cloud decision-making. By benchmarking each entity and the group as a whole, the accountant provided clarity, accountability, and a roadmap that improved both profits and family harmony.

www.ingramcontent.com/pod-product-compliance
Lightning Source LLC
Chambersburg PA
CBHW042116190326
41519CB00030B/7514